lonely planet

KU-711-747

# LOS ANGELES

## ENCOUNTER

**AMY C. BALFOUR**

Los Angeles Encounter

**Published by Lonely Planet Publications Pty Ltd**
ABN 36 005 607 983

| | |
|---|---|
| **Australia** | Head Office, Locked Bag 1, Footscray, Vic 3011 <br> ☎ 03 8379 8000  fax 03 8379 8111 <br> talk2us@lonelyplanet.com.au |
| **USA** | 150 Linden St, Oakland, CA 94607 <br> ☎ 510 893 8555 <br> toll free 800 275 8555 <br> fax 510 893 8572 <br> info@lonelyplanet.com |
| **UK** | 72–82 Rosebery Ave, Clerkenwell, London EC1R 4RW <br> ☎ 020 7841 9000  fax 020 7841 9001 <br> go@lonelyplanet.co.uk |

This title was commissioned in Lonely Planet's Oakland office and produced by: **Commissioning Editor** Suki Gear **Coordinating Editors** Kate James, Sarah Stewart **Coordinating Cartographer** Owen Eszeki **Assisting Cartographers** Csanad Csutoros, Joshua Geoghegan, Andy Rojas **Layout Designer** David Kemp **Senior Editor** Helen Christinis **Managing Cartographer** Alison Lyall **Cover Designer** Brendan Dempsey **Project Manager** Rachel Imeson **Series Designer** Wendy Wright **Thanks to** Sally Darmody, Jennifer Garrett, Michelle Glynn, Laura Jane, Paul Piaia, Raphael Richards, Vivek Wagle, Celia Wood

**Cover photograph** Surfing at Hermosa Beach pier, Christina Lease/Lonely Planet Images. **Internal photographs** p58, p76, p90, p102 by Amy C. Balfour; p11 Warner Brothers Entertainment. All other photographs by David Peevers except p4, p18, p27, p29, p42, p71 p83, p86, p120 p168, p169, p170 p174, p175 Ray Laskowitz; p151 Richard Cummins; p157 Hanan Isachar; p176 Richard I'Anson.

All images are copyright of the photographers unless otherwise indicated. Many of the images in this guide are available for licensing from **Lonely Planet Images:** www.lonelyplanetimages.com.

ISBN 978 1 74104 790 5

Printed through Colorcraft Ltd, Hong Kong.

Printed in China

# HOW TO USE THIS BOOK
## Color-Coding & Maps

Color-coding is used for symbols on maps and the text that they relate to (eg all eating venues on the maps and in the text are given a green knife and fork symbol). Each neighborhood also gets its own color, and this is used down the edge of the page and throughout that neighborhood section.

Shaded yellow areas on the maps denote 'areas of interest' — for their historical significance, their attractive architecture or their great bars and restaurants. We encourage you to head to these areas and just start exploring!

## AMY C. BALFOUR

Amy arrived in Los Angeles by way of Virginia where she'd been a deskbound attorney living her life in six-minute billable increments. Hearing the call of Hollywood, she chucked a stable salary and health insurance to break in as a screenwriter. After a stint reviewing legal documents in downtown LA, she accepted a writer's assistant gig with NBC's *Law & Order* and learned how one-hour TV dramas are produced. She was eventually reprimanded for leading security on a low-speed golf-cart chase through the restricted NBC/Universal Studios backlot after an unauthorized tour. She's

lived in Manhattan Beach and Mid-City, hiked the Santa Monica Mountains, attended celeb-filled screenings, navigated the velvet rope, and sampled margaritas all over town. Amy recently jumped from TV into full-time freelancing, and has written for the *Los Angeles Times*, *Every Day with Rachael Ray*, *Women's Health*, *Backpacker* and *Travelers' Tales*.

## AMY'S THANKS

Thanks to the many friends who shared their LA expertise. Particularly awesome were Chris P, Allison, Vid, Karen, Lisa, Sheila, David and the L&O gang. Special thanks to Suki Gear for her unflagging support and patient assistance and the Peevers for many helpful pointers. Thanks to Sara Benson for her work on *Best of Los Angeles*.

## THE PHOTOGRAPHER

David Peevers (www.peevers-la.com) is a photographer, writer and adventurer whose work has appeared in many Lonely Planet books and countless international publications and websites. He has been a whitewater river guide, a blue-water sailor, a publisher of tribal Indian art and special-projects manager for the *Los Angeles Business Journal*. A citizen of the US and Ireland, he has lived in Los Angeles with his wife, Lonely Planet author Andrea Schulte-Peevers, since 1984 and is planning an imminent move to their favorite city, Berlin.

---

**Our Readers** Many thanks to the travelers who wrote to us with helpful hints, useful advice and interesting anecdotes: Miriam Cullen, Sue Davis, Lubna Debbini, Donal Doyle, Dusty, Joshua Grubaugh, Amy Luczak, Karen Mundy, Betty Pasley, Bernadette Sanz, BJ Semmes, Jason Vorders, Lydia Welton, Brian Yates.

Bold as brass on the Walk of Fame (p43)

# CONTENTS

# THIS IS LOS ANGELES

Welcome to sunny Los Angeles, a shiny city of reinvention where small talk always starts with a question: 'Where are you from?' This query shows what's behind the city's energetic buzz – a perpetual in-flow of dreamers, go-getters and hustlers primed with unabashed optimism.

Where else could an English acrobat named Archibald Leach become debonair Cary Grant? Or an Austrian bodybuilder lift his way from Muscle Beach to the governor's mansion? Even the water's from someplace else, imported almost a century ago after DWP chief William Mulholland opened the gates of his 233-mile aqueduct and millions of gallons rushed into the city. His words to the crowd? 'There it is. Take it.'

The crowd took, and the hustle hasn't stopped since. Screenwriters pitch in the shadows of the Hollywood sign. Surfers squint for the choicest Malibu wave. Then there are the true dream-chasers, the eternal optimists who join the line at Pink's – willing to wait hours for a bite of the perfect chili dog.

Don't care for hotdogs? A few steps away are the healthy macrobiotic delights of M Café de Chaya, where a hot dog would be met with gasps of Juicy Coutured horror. But that's LA – a bustling mash-up of culture, community and cuisine, where clubs-du-jour lurk beside old-school delis, ramshackle markets wobble near gleaming malls, palm trees sway over car-carrying rivers, and renowned museums preen beside bubbling tar pits.

As for the city portrayed in Oscar-winning *Crash*, LA's not quite so angry – everybody's too busy chattering on cells, checking Blackberries or downward dogging to worry about the next guy. Unless it's a casting agent, of course. Yes, the city runs a little thick on superficiality, self-absorption and sunshine, but c'mon, isn't that the point? Have fun. Reinvent. Shop. Hike. Surf. Party. LA is yours to grab. To paraphrase Mulholland: 'There it is. Go for it.'

---

**Top left** Frank Gehry's striking Walt Disney Concert Hall (p129) **Top right** Strutting in stars and stripes, Muscle Beach (p20)
**Bottom** Glamour and gloss in the Hollywood Museum (p42)

# >HIGHLIGHTS

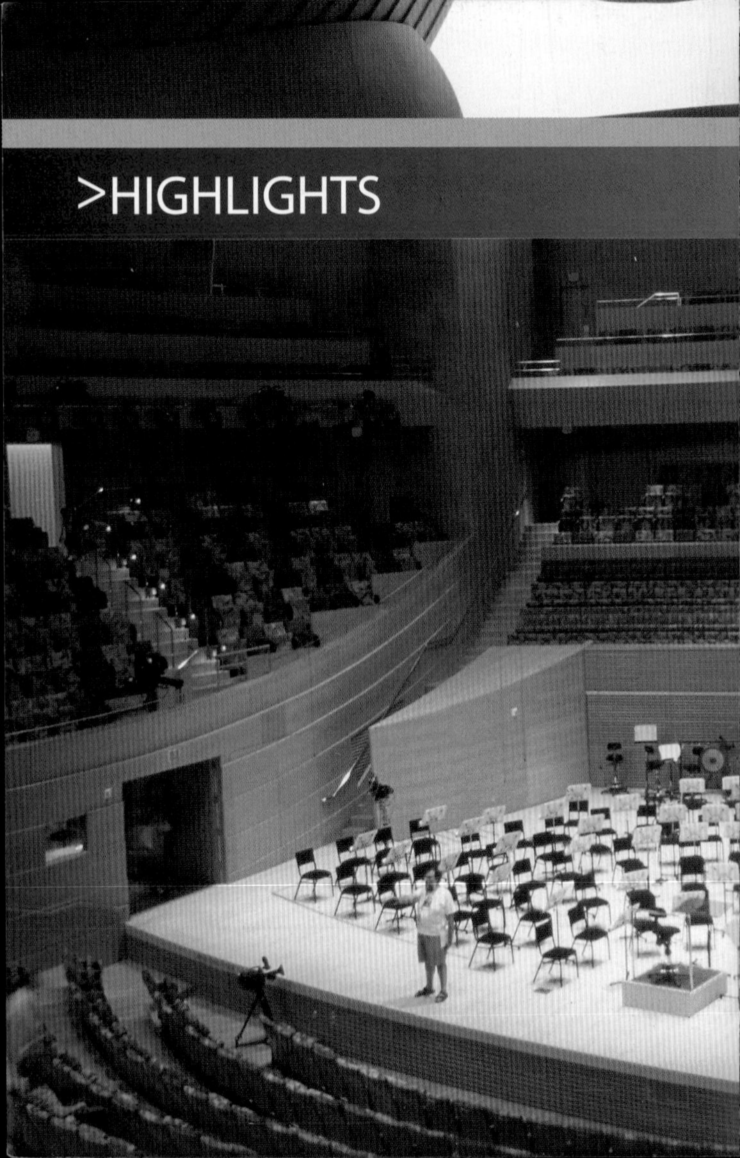

The internal organs of the Walt Disney Concert Hall (p14)

# > 1 WARNER BROS STUDIO TOUR

## SQUIRM UNDER THE SORTING HAT ON THE WARNER BROS TOUR

Gryffindor? Hufflepuff? Which Hogwarts house is meant for you? At Warner Bros memorabilia museum, fans of JK Rowling suffer their fate under the talking Sorting Hat, the primo attraction at the studio's top-notch Harry Potter exhibit. Goblets of Fire, giant spiders and gargantuan costumes – not to mention The Cupboard Under The Stairs – pack the museum's 2nd floor, usually the last stop on the 2¼-hour VIP tour that winds past sound stages, sitcom sets and historical sights on the studio's sprawling Burbank lot.

Overshadowed by the flashy behemoth down the road (more commonly known as Universal Studios; p137), Warner Bros offers low-key, more personal wows. Instead of rides, explosions and giant rubber sharks, you'll get an up-close look at the sets and stages currently used for TV dramas and sitcoms. Guides encourage questions and provide specific answers. Did you know it takes a week to shoot a one-hour drama? That ceilings aren't shown on most shows because the space is filled with lights and lamps? Sets where you'll learn these behind-the-scenes secrets include *ER*, *The Gilmore Girls*, *George Lopez*, and *Two and a Half Men* – the availability depends on shooting schedules.

Trams wind through the 110-acre lot, meandering through faux suburban neighborhoods, a town square and urban row houses – yep, that's the ladder where an upside-down Spidey kissed Mary Jane. Everyone unloads at the Transportation Garage for Bruce Wayne's tricked-out Batmobile from *Batman Begins* and Scooby's psychedelic Mystery Machine. Nearby, the *Friends'* coffee shop, Central Perk, is forever preserved for your picture-taking, couch-sitting pleasure.

Though not guaranteed, celebrity-spotting potential is better than average. As the tram continues past massive sound stages, it's not uncommon to see a recognizable face heading to his or her trailer. However, fall, winter and early spring may be best for star-spotting, since most shows shut down in May for hiatus. But be warned, jumping off the tram for a celebrity hug is strongly discouraged (although

stars – Tom Cruise for one – have popped onto trams for impromptu fan-lovin').

Back at the museum, you've got 20 minutes to snoop – from Dr Kovac's lab coat to Earl Hamner's typewriter to Wonder Woman's flashy unitard, there are movie and TV costumes, scripts and props galore. And as for the Sorting Hat, if Slytherin's your house, don't worry, you're allowed a second take. See also p140.

# >2 HOLLYWOOD

## ENJOY DINNER AND A MOVIE WITH HOLLYWOOD STARS

If you don't have anything nice to say, well, you're probably talking about Hollywood & Highland (p42). Love it or hate it, this cornerside patch of excess – opened in 2001 – was a pivotal first step in Hollywood's long-overdue makeover. More Botox injection than subtle tuck, however, the towering complex is considered by some to be a bloated five-story mishmash of megashopping, movie-themed kitsch, meandering humanity and garish excess. But then again, isn't that the point? The place does bring in the masses, and revenues are reportedly rising.

So how to find the romance of Hollywood? Those in the know do it the old-fashioned way with dinner and a movie. Tasty dining options abound: lush salads at Wolfgang Puck's Vert (p46), juicy burgers at the Bowery (p47), oh-so-fresh seafood at the Hungry Cat (p44) and Asian with-a-kick at Kung Pao Kitty (p45). Outside, the brass stars of favorite celebs line Hollywood Blvd's Walk of Fame (p43), where you can also catch a ride on the looping Holly Trolley (boxed text, p48), which will whisk you to the theater of your choice – or somewhere very close by.

The state-of-the-art ArcLight Cinemas (p48) draw moviegoers willing to pay a bit more for preselected seats. Locals love the proximity of massive indie music store Amoeba Music (p43), not to mention the eclectic mix of movie tomes in the theatre's gift-store lobby. There's one-stop shopping a few blocks away at Cinespace (p49), where dinner, a movie and late-night dancing are the weekend triple feature. For quirky retrospectives, check www.egyptiantheatre .com to see what's unfurling at Sid Grauman's 1922 Egyptian Theatre (p50), Hollywood's oldest movie palace. Two blocks west is Grauman's Chinese Theatre (p39), the ornate grand dame of Hollywood movie palaces. Those approaching her dragon-draped doors must first elbow past the yawping hordes marveling over footprints left by yesterday's stars in the concrete courtyard (I'll admit, Judy Garland's are ridiculously small). Inside, spend a moment in the powder room or men's lounge imagining the hundreds of stars and moviegoers that have preened at the very same mirror.

A word of caution – the celebrity impersonators on the sidewalk outside Grauman's Chinese Theatre are independent operators hoping to get cash for photos. Chewbacca was recently arrested for head-butting an intrusive tour guide. The perp's alleged last words? 'Nobody tells this wookiee what to do!'

# >3 WALT DISNEY CONCERT HALL

## ADMIRE THE ARCHITECTURAL WONDER OF THE WALT DISNEY CONCERT HALL

Billowing sail? Blooming rose? No one knows exactly what architect Frank Gehry had in mind – and he's not telling – when he designed the Walt Disney Concert Hall, now preening like a silver ribbon atop downtown's Bunker Hill. Completed in 2003, the structure of stainless-steel panels – 6664 to be precise – was an instant iconic addition to the downtown landscape.

But no large-scale architectural project goes unexamined, and the concert hall had its share of controversies during its 16-year journey to completion. The building was initiated by a $50 million dollar gift to the LA Music Center by Walt Disney's widow Lillian, but design changes, funding delays and neighborhood concerns hampered its progress. And the neighbors may have had a point. Reflective glare from the shiny panels reportedly melted traffic cones, blinded drivers and raised the temperature in surrounding apartments at least 10 degrees. A last-minute buffing project – on offending panels only – did the trick and the hall was finally complete. Total cost? Estimates range from $275 million to $300 million.

Inside and out, it's the astounding but subtle attention to detail and form that impresses most – smooth Douglas fir columns hide air-conditioning units, sloping Gehry-designed fonts blend into curving walls, and specially smashed pieces of Lillian's favorite porcelain personalize her rose-shaped memorial fountain. Even LA's car-obsessed citizenry wasn't forgotten – guests are whisked up silent, cascading escalators directly from the garage into the main lobby. The auditorium itself, unfortunately, isn't typically accessible during the daily architectural or garden tours. The LA Phil uses the space for rehearsals, and in the acoustically precise performance hall there are no minor distractions allowed.

With only minimal preplanning, however, it's possible to enjoy the perfect blend of music and architecture. After completing the last guided tour or self-directed audio-tour (www.musiccenter.org/vtc/toursched.html; p129), linger over cocktails and fine food at Water Grill (p133), R23 (p133) or one of the many downtown restaurants

accessible by the Music Center Shuttle (boxed text, p130). After dinner, mingle with a diverse, well-dressed crowd – but nothing too fancy – in the hall's flowing lobbies. Once inside the 2265-seat inner sanctum, which looks much like the majestic hull of a finely crafted ship, settle in for an unparalleled sensory celebration and one of LA's finest encounters. See also p129.

# >4 THE GETTY CENTER

## CATCH A PORTRAIT-WORTHY SUNSET AT THE GETTY CENTER

No matter where you stand on the Getty's sweeping southeast plaza, the sunset view is worthy of an Old Master portrait (or an impressionist on smoggy days). The Pacific, the San Gabriels, even 405 brake lights, flicker with a more sublime glow when framed by travertine stone. And this merging of nature and culture is exactly what architect Richard Meier had in mind when designing the 110-acre campus terracing up the side of the Santa Monica foothills.

Since its opening in 1997, more than 10 million visitors have boarded driverless trams for a scenic glide to the Getty's sprawling arrival plaza. From there, a natural flow of walkways, skylights and courtyards encourages effortless wanderings between galleries, gardens and outdoor cafés. Although scandals cast shadows across sun-dappled terraces in 2006 (the arrest of the antiquities curator and the resignation of the Porsche-driving Getty Trust president), recent unpleasantness can't detract from the paintings, manuscripts, drawings and photographs comprising the heart of the permanent collection.

For maximizing your Getty experience, try Friday afternoon just before sunset. Once a month, free 'Fridays off the 405' lure visitors with outdoor concerts, but the rest are quieter. Sip wine on the terrace, wander over a flower-lined stream to the Central Garden, or simply prop your elbows on a travertine ledge – somewhere the perfect sunset awaits. See also p83.

# >5 ABBOT KINNEY BOULEVARD

## SHOP THE BUSTLING SIDEWALKS OF VENICE'S ABBOT KINNEY BOULEVARD

At the turn of the 20th century, tobacco heir Abbot Kinney won ownership of Venice Beach on the flip of a coin, subsequently using luck, vision and entrepreneurial know-how to turn a 1½-mile strip of marshland into a profitable seaside resort. Kinney lured the masses with Venetian-style buildings, theme-park rides and a series of artificial canals filled with water, gondolas and imported gondoliers from Italy.

Though most of the canals were eventually paved, Kinney's bohemian spirit remains, not only along the Venice Ocean Front Walk (p20), but also in the vibrant array of charming boutiques, locally owned restaurants and laid-back bars that line his namesake boulevard where there's nary a McDonald's or Gap to be found.

Abbot Kinney runs southwest from Main St with most stores clustered between Westminster Ave and North Venice Blvd. Pamper your inner foodie with a wide array of culinary delights – tasty tapas at Primitivo Wine Bistro (p114), savory slices at Abbot's Pizza (p112), primo Cal-French at Joe's (p113) and sinful sweets at Three Square Bakery & Café (p114). Stylistas can indulge their fashion habit with beach-chic flair at Firefly (p111) and London looks at Brick Lane (p110), or discover something unexpected at the numerous boutiques dotting these boho blocks. Guys can flip through surfing and architecture books at bike-friendly Equator Books (p111). From food to fashion to footwear, funky Abbot Kinney is a first choice for indie-minded shoppers.

# > 6 PACIFIC COAST HIGHWAY

## CRUISE THE PACIFIC COAST HIGHWAY IN A CONVERTIBLE

Shades on? Check. Top down? Check. Tank full of gas? Yes? So what are you hanging around for? Thirty miles of sun-kissed California highway awaits. Start your engines on the Pacific Coast Hwy (PCH) northwest of the Santa Monica Pier and don't stop 'til you reach Point Magu. With the Pacific on your left and the Santa Monica Mountains on your right, you've got all the map you need.

A lot flashes past – around Malibu (boxed text, p104) there's the revamped Getty Villa, Surfrider Beach and the exclusive Malibu Colony. Soon it's the sun-dappled slopes of Pepperdine University, one of America's prettiest campuses. Then Zuma Beach's wide beaches – and the buff bodies that love them – beckon like surfside sirens. Up next is rocky El Matador – once a fave of nude sunbathers – followed by the tidepools of Leo Carillo.

As mini-malls drop away, two-wheeled travelers swoop in – bright, lycra-clad cyclists line the road's shoulders while longhaired easy riders roar up in the rearview. But all stop for Neptune's Net, a wide-porched sanctuary serving up clam chowder and cold brews.

Just ahead is scrubby Mugu Peak, looming over La Jolla Canyon and the western terminus of the Backbone Trail – which began its run 30 miles back, too. Pull over, take it in – playful seals, migrating whales and, if it's clear, the Channel Islands. Linger or return – it's all good.

# >7 GRIFFITH OBSERVATORY

## CONTEMPLATE THE BIG PICTURE AT THE GRIFFITH OBSERVATORY

Billions and billions of stars for millions and millions of dollars. And judging from the hordes clamoring to catch a starry glimpse, the Griffith Observatory's recent $93 million makeover was money well spent. By the 1990s, the earthquake-proof observatory (p54), a gift to the city from mining mogul Griffith J Griffith in 1935, had been fading into a black hole of irrelevance, and was perhaps best known as the site of James Dean's angst-ridden, planetary musings in *Rebel Without a Cause*.

Today the revamped Oschin Planetarium houses the Zeiss Universarium Mark IX – the world's most advanced star projector. Nearby, the Cosmic Connection drops you in front of the Big Picture – a floor-to-ceiling digital image of a sliver of the universe bursting with galaxies, stars and lurking dark matter. Elsewhere, Tesla's sizzling coil and nine planetary scales (ladies, go for Mercury) offer more tangible thrills.

Outside, savor stunning balcony views of the Hollywood Hills and the gleaming city below. Views of surrounding Griffith Park may be somewhat less stunning after the fire that raged through in May 2007. Have your picture snapped beside the haunting bust of James Dean, the Hollywood sign caught neatly in the background. Inside, even infinity can't escape the long arm of Wolfgang Puck – his Café at the End of the Universe (p59) offers tortilla soup for the universe-weary soul.

HIGHLIGHTS

# >8 OCEAN FRONT WALK

## MUSCLE YOUR WAY THROUGH THE MOBS IN VENICE

For $5 a day, pasty cubicle-jockeys can channel their inner Arnold Schwarzenegger. All it takes is a trip to 'the Pit' at Muscle Beach, Venice – look for the massive concrete barbells – along with a dollop of attitude. It'll be needed among the shaved heads, rippling torsos and grunting bench-pressers at this outdoor testosterone fest.

If public weightlifting isn't your thing, don't despair. There are plenty of ways to get your freak on at the mile-long strip of in-your-face exuberance known as the Venice Beach Boardwalk (see also p110). The rabbit-hole's landing pad is the intersection of Ocean Front and Windward, where your senses get their full bohemian fix. Psychedelic storefronts. Bongo beats. Pungent incense. Sizzling samples of Jody Maroni's (p112). The bump and nudge of attitudinous skate-rats. It all whizzes past in a Technicolor blur of performers, vendors, bums, tattoo artists and paddleball players.

There are oases of calm. Step into friendly Small World Books (p112) for conversation or a beach read. If art's your angle, try the cool, contemporary LA Louver (p110), where you might catch David Hockney's latest. For soccer talk and Erdinger Weizenbier, grab a seat on the rowdy international patio at On the Waterfront Cafe (p115). Before that first sip, appreciate the view that started it all – surf, sand and sun-loving palms. And maybe that turbaned roller-skating guy.

# >9 LA BREA TAR PITS & MUSEUM ROW

**EXPLORE THE LA BREA TAR PITS, LA'S GOOEY UNDERBELLY**

It's impossible to drive by the La Brea Tar Pits (p71) without turning for a look. Yep, that's a big black pool of crude oil percolating beside Wilshire Blvd. But don't run off the road considering the symbolism. Instead, park and stroll over to the main pit (it's free), where a life-sized replica of a giant mammoth roars from the ensnaring tar – a startling but tragic example of the dangers of wandering too close. Follow the sidewalk to Pit 91 to watch paleontologists remove prehistoric bones from the depths of the muck (July to early September). Inside at the Page Museum, ponder reconstructed bones of these mammoths, mastodons and menacing saber-toothed cats. While some sniff that the holograms, tar pull and dioramic beasts are old school, please note that one man's cheesy is another man's retro.

What else lingers near the bubbling goo? Tens of thousands of priceless works of art. That's right, the Los Angeles County Museum of Art (LACMA; p71) borders the ever-present tar pits. Brilliant juxtaposition or a breathtaking lack of foresight? No matter – the wide-ranging collections of European paintings, Islamic and Southeast Asian art and contemporary masterpieces will certainly distract you. If Bugattis, Batmobiles and motorized buggies are more your speed, cross Wilshire Blvd to the Petersen Automotive Museum (p74), a car-buff's paradise.

# >10 MANHATTAN & HERMOSA

## BREAKFAST AND BIKE IN THE SOUTH BAY

There's always a line at Uncle Bill's Pancake House (p122) in Manhattan Beach. And not just any line. Nope, this line consists of some of the most attractive people in the Western Hemisphere, all waiting for the same thing: scrumptious omelets, towering pancakes and over-stuffed wraps. Even Quentin Tarantino, master of kung-fu irony and grindhouse gore, loves the vibe at this sunny breakfast paradise.

Uncle Bill's isn't the only hotspot south of LAX. From Manhattan Beach to Hermosa and Redondo, the South Bay is the place to be, the recent rise in teardowns, real-estate prices and trendy restaurants serving as unofficial indicators. See for yourself on the South Bay Bike Path, colloquially called The Strand, as it rolls through quintessential LA beach country – it's all surfboards, volleyball, bikinis and boardshorts in this shimmering seaside part of town.

At Manhattan Beach, grab a Fun Bunn's (p118) cruiser for a lazy, traffic-free glide south. On clear days, Catalina Island beckons, counterbalancing the bright blue frivolity of the 90210 house – its exterior instantly recognizable as Kelly and Brenda's beach pad from the Aaron Spelling classic. Dogwalkers, stroller-moms and skate-rats share the path in Hermosa, known locally as a breeding ground for future reality stars. Pedal slowly and flash your best smile – you might just find yourself on the next Mark Burnett juggernaut.

# >11 DOWNTOWN FASHION DISTRICT

## SHOP IN A BARGAIN-LOVER'S PARADISE

Nordstrom's semiannual sale. Barney's warehouse blowout. All mere child's play to serious LA bargain shoppers. They save their best game for downtown's Fashion District – a 90-block trove of stores and stalls where discount shopping is an Olympian sport. Jewelry, jeans, purses, shoes, designer knock-offs – you name it, they're hawking it in this mazelike warren of 1000 stores. Smack in the middle of it all is tiny Santee Alley, catnip for frugal fashionistas – its high-energy mix of jam-packed stalls, bustling vendors and boombox beats lures in discount divers for that one-of-a-kind find.

Bounded by 7th St to the north and the Santa Monica Fwy to the south, the main throughline is Los Angeles St. Women's wear clusters around Santee Alley while men's casuals, kids' wear and accessories fill outer blocks. Map glancing is expected (www.fashiondistrict.org), but once you're oriented it's easy to shop like a local: bring cash, avoid stores where 'solo mayoreo' or 'wholesale only' hangs in the window, and know that dressing rooms aren't the norm. As for haggling, it might be part of the thrill but prices are so low, don't expect much of a cut. Embrace the vastness of it all, and let the shopping games begin! See also p130.

# >12 DISNEYLAND

## WANDER THE HAPPIEST PLACE ON EARTH

If you're unhappy at Disneyland, you have no one to blame but yourself. From the moment you board the cheery tram, there's a perceptible change in atmosphere. Wide-eyed children lean forward while stressed-out parents relax. Uncle Walt's in charge, and he's covered every possible detail.

A bright floral Mickey greets visitors at the entrance, enticing everyone toward Main St USA, where there's a parade every day of the week. From Adventureland to Fantasyland to Tomorrowland, every attraction, restaurant and cast member has been carefully crafted to conform to Disney's grand illusion.

There are a few potholes on Main St – most rides seem to end in a gift store, prices are high, and there are grumblings that management could do more to ensure affordable local housing for employees. But even the most-determined Nietzsche-quoting malcontent will find something to warrant a smile. For one, Mr Toad continues his slightly boozy Wild Ride to nowhere in particular, spared the fate of his squashed Disney World counterpart. Smoking isn't completely banned – see the jittery crew huddled behind the Matterhorn. Finally, there's the apocryphal story of the villainous sculptor: stand west of the central 'Partners' statue of Walt and Mickey and look toward Tomorrowland. The position of Mickey's bulbous nose makes it appear that Uncle Walt is, in fact, *very* happy to see you. But you didn't hear it from me. See also p152.

# >LOS ANGELES CALENDAR

Diversity isn't just a political buzzword in Los Angeles, it's another excuse to party. And the best part is, everyone's invited. From banjos to bongos, film fests to book fairs, Day of the Dead to Doo Dah, it's nonstop celebrating all year long. And that's without mentioning WeHo's hedonistic Halloween hootenanny, drawing half a million costumed revelers. If you can't find something to do, you ain't looking. For a monthly listing of citywide events see www.culturela.org. Art aficionados get their tips from www.artscenecal.com or check Thursday calendar listings from the *LA Times* and *LA Weekly*. Otherwise, look online at www.laweekly.com, www.calendarlive.com or www.dailycandy.com for upcoming fun.

Flower-filled floats at the yearly Tournament of Roses (p26)

# JANUARY

## Tournament of Roses

☎ 626-449-4100; www.tournamentof roses.com

Everyone loves a parade, and this 2½-hour cavalcade of flower-festooned floats just before Pasadena's Rose Bowl is one of the most beloved. Die-hards camp out to snag prime sidewalk spots. Otherwise, avoid traffic, take the metro to Memorial Park and hoof it in.

# FEBRUARY

## Chinese New Year

☎ 213-680-0243; www.lachinese chamber.org

Colorful celebrations in Chinatown mark the lunar new year, culminating in the Golden Dragon parade, food, floats, fashion and firecrackers. Late January/early February.

## Pan African Film & Arts Festival

☎ 323-295-1706; www.paff.org

Catch a flick at America's largest black film festival during Black History month. Entrants from the US, Africa, Europe, South America and beyond.

## Academy Awards

☎ 310-247-3000; www.oscars .org/bleachers

Ogle your favorite film stars from the Kodak Theatre's red-carpet-adjacent bleachers. Apply in September for one of 600 lucky spots.

# MARCH

## LA Marathon

☎ 310-444-5544; www.lamarathon.com

Rally the runners then wander past performance stages and finish-line festivities. It's a 26.2-mile party through the city — for the one million spectators, that is.

## Blessing of the Animals

☎ 213-485-8372; www.cityofla.org

From Chihuahuas to iguanas, all critters welcome for Cardinal Mahoney's blessing at this fun-loving Olvera St fest on the Saturday before Easter.

Colorful celebrations at Chinese New Year

Finesse unfurled at the Fiesta Broadway

## APRIL

### LA Festival of Books

☎ 213-237-7335; www.latimes.com/
extras/festivalofbooks
It's a bookworm's paradise for two days at
UCLA. Revel in reading with 400 authors,
300 booths, 97 panels and 130,000
bibliophiles.

### Toyota Grand Prix of Long Beach

☎ 888-827-7333; www.longbeachgp.com
World-class drivers tear through city streets
on temporary tracks at this week-long racing
spectacle by the sea.

## MAY

### Venice Art Fair

www.venicefamilyclinic.org
Art, architecture, auctions and studio tours
to benefit the Venice Family Clinic.

### Topanga Banjo Fiddle Contest & Folk Festival

☎ 818-382-4819; www.topanga
banjofiddle.org
Toe-tappin' bluegrass and old-time tunes
tear up the Malibu hills.

### Fiesta Broadway

☎ 310-914-8308; www.fiestabroadway.la
Watch 500,000 flock to downtown for the
world's largest Cinco de Mayo celebration.

LOS ANGELES CALENDAR

Pride on parade at LA Pridefest

## JUNE

### LA Pridefest
☎ 323-969-8302; www.lapride.org
The rainbow starts on Santa Monica Blvd
for two days of love, equality and pride at
Christopher St West's GBLT party. About
300,000 show for the parade.

### LA Film Festival
☎ 866-345-6337; www.lafilmfest.com
It's a movieable feast – 175 movies, 10 days,
80,000 film lovers. Feed your inner fanboy
with documentaries, shorts and features.

## JULY

### July 4th
www.rosebowlstadium.com, www
.hollywoodbowl.com, www.beaches
.co.la.ca.us
Follow the fireworks to celebrate America's
independence. From Pasadena's Rose Bowl
extravaganza to the Hollywood Bowl's
symphonic sounds to Marina del Rey's
seaside spectacular, start looking to the
skies at 9:00pm.

## AUGUST

### Manhattan Beach 6-Man Volleyball Tournament
☎ 310-802-5413; www.surffestival.org
Beers, bikinis, costumes and volleyballs –
all on tap at this whacked-out volleyball
fest where teams with themes set spikes on
the beach.

### Nisei Week Japanese Festival
☎ 213-687-7193; www.niseiweek.org
Created during the Great Depression to lift
spirits, this nine-day Little Tokyo celebration
features floral arrangements, tea ceremonies
and calligraphy.

# SEPTEMBER

### LA County Fair
☎ 909-623-3111; www.lacountyfair.com
Monster trucks, rock'n'roll, pie-eating contests, a Ferris wheel and cows. 'Nuff said.

### Nautica Malibu Triathlon
☎ 818-707-8867; www.nautica malibutri.com
It's swim, bike, run for celebs and top triathletes at booth- and body-filled Zuma Beach.

### Watts Towers Day of the Drum & Jazz Festivals
☎ 213-847-4646; www.wattstowers.org
Multicultural beats — Japanese, African, Native American, Latin — draw fans partial to percussion.

# OCTOBER

### West Hollywood Halloween Carnaval
☎ 323-848-6400; www.weho.org, www.visitwesthollyood.com
Leave your inhibitions at home for this over-the-top costume extravaganza drawing half a million party people to the streets of WeHo. Leather and lace, togas and flip-flops, queens, ghouls and cowboys — free your costume fantasies. Music, food, comedians and a costume contest are icing on the carnival cake.

Inspired Watts Towers, home to Day of the Drum & Jazz Festivals

## SPECIAL EVENTS ON A REGULAR BASIS

**Downtown Artwalk** (www.downtownartwalk.com) More than 25 galleries and museums participate in this increasingly popular art ramble held the second Thursday of every month from noon to 9pm.

**Grand Performances** (www.grandperformances.org) From late June through early October, catch free concerts from international artists in the California Plaza in the heart of the financial district.

# NOVEMBER

### Dia de los Muertos Festival

www.olvera-street.com

Honor beloved ancestors with dance, face painting and nightly processions at this weeklong Mexican remembrance.

### Pasadena Doo Dah Parade

☎ 626-205-4029; www.pasadena doodahparade.info

Embrace this wacky parody parade. With its briefcase drill team, Royal Pains and 'howdy krishnas,' it's a tongue-in-cheek poke at Rose Bowl perfection. Sunday before Thanksgiving.

# DECEMBER

### Griffith Park Light Festival

☎ 323-913-4688; www.laparks.org

Bright lights, no city in this mile-long drive through Griffith Park's colorful holiday light displays, from late November through December 26.

### Marina del Rey Holiday Boat Parade

☎ 310-670-7130; www.mdrboatparade .org

Boats decked out in bright, blinking, holiday cheer promenade for prizes in the marina. Check it out from Fisherman's Village.

Night lights at the Egyptian Theatre (p50)

# ITINERARIES

LA is a tourists' mecca – from Hollywood to the beaches to the museums, there's always a tantalizing choice around the bend. But resist the temptation to over-schedule. Traffic can turn a 2-mile trip into a two-hour detour at the drop of a mattress from an oversized truck. If traffic happens, don't stress. Call it quintessential LA and readjust the plan.

## DAY ONE

Grab breakfast at the Griddle Café (p66) then head to Warner Bros Studio (p140) for a morning tour. Next up it's Hollywood & Highland (p42), the Walk of Fame (p43), and historic footprints at Grauman's Chinese Theatre (p39). Grab lunch at Vert (p46) then off to shop Melrose Ave or Rodeo Dr. Enjoy a martini at celeb-heavy Polo Lounge (p93) then it's AOC (p78) or Koi (p66) for dinner. Cap it off with late-night laughs, music or movies in Hollywood.

## DAY TWO

Enjoy primo people-watching over lattes at Abbot's Habit (p115), then browse the stores of Abbot Kinney Blvd. For beach time, hit over-the-top Venice Beach (p108) or slightly quieter Santa Monica (p94). Then it's art and maybe a sunset at the Getty Center (p83). For dinner, consider rowdy Mexican at El Cholo (p103) or savory sushi at the Hump (p104). Sip mojitos seaside at the Lobster (p105) for a nightcap.

Tar treasure – a mastodon skeleton at the Page Museum (p71)

## FORWARD PLANNING

For Disneyland, make hotel reservations as soon as you know trip dates, since many hotels fill fast for peak times. Order park admission tickets a few months ahead of time too.

Otherwise, a month's preplanning should suffice. Familiarize yourself with the city's layout to best organize your time. Peruse www.calendarlive.com, www.laweekly.com, www.artscenela.com and www.dailycandy.com to see what's on tap at museums, restaurants, performance halls and galleries. It's best to double-check museum websites – many are closed Mondays, and some may have renovation-based closings. If a performance of the LA Phil at the Walt Disney Concert Hall (p129) is a must-do, order tickets online. Calendars for specific venues such as the Hollywood Bowl (p51), the Greek Theatre (p61) and the Hotel Café (p51) appear online a few months ahead of showtime.

Two weeks out, make reservations at the more popular restaurants. Weekends are toughest, but primo nights for celeb sightings at dining hotspots are actually Tuesday through Thursday. Think ahead for popular comedy clubs such as the Comedy & Magic Club (p123), though most improv performances have availability on show night. Book tickets to the Warner Bros Studio tour (p140), check online deals for Universal Studios (p137), and nab live studio audience tickets (boxed text, p140).

One day out? Pack your shades, shorts, sandals and sunscreen.

## DAY THREE

Fuel up at Toast (p80) or Doughboys (p78) then boogie to Griffith Park (p52) for planets (p54), cowboys (p56) and monkeys (p55), or try Wilshire's Museum Row for art (p71), cars (p74) and tar (p71). Up next is an afternoon tour of the Walt Disney Concert Hall (p129) with a stop by the Museum of Contemporary Art (p64). Enjoy a fine dinner then hop a music shuttle for an evening performance at the concert hall. If the line's not crazy, zip up to the Standard rooftop bar (p134) for stellar city views.

## FOR FREE

Excluding the cost of transportation and parking, you can see LA's best without spending a dime. Museum-wise, the Getty Center is always free, LACMA is free after 5pm, and most others offer one free day a month. Enjoy Hollywood at no cost too – wander Hollywood Blvd's Walk of Fame (p43), then loiter in the courtyard at Grauman's Chinese Theatre (p39), then snag free audience tickets for a sitcom taping (boxed text, p140) or stroll celeb-filled Hollywood Forever Cemetery (p39). To get a feel for the city as a whole, drive west on Sunset Blvd from downtown all the way to the Pacific. Once you're at the beach, park and enjoy a scenic seaside stroll.

Multitasking LA-style at Venice Beach (p108)

# NEIGHBORHOODS

Yes, the rumors are true, you really can surf in the morning and ski in the afternoon – traffic gods and snow-pack willing. But seriously, why rush through town, not to mention a complete wardrobe change, when there's so much to do right here?

Seekers of surf and sand have their pick of primo beaches with sparkling swaths stretching from Malibu to Santa Monica to the South Bay. Hollywood hounds have distractions equally as numerous – from tell-all tram tours in Burbank to historical strolls along the Walk of Fame to celeb-spotting in Mid-City, you'll get your 15 minutes. Or at least somebody else's. You want a little culture? Try downtown's fine stash of museums, music halls and architectural landmarks, not to mention proximity to Pasadena's stellar trove as well. And shopping? Every neighborhood's got a strong sense of self sharply reflected in its shopping districts – beachy and chic in Santa Monica, trendy and tiny on Melrose Ave, funky and fashion-forward in Venice, arts- and design-minded in West Hollywood, and ever-so-posh on Beverly Hills' Rodeo Dr. And that's without mentioning deals galore in downtown's Fashion District.

As for nightlife, pound the pavement on Sunset Strip for a mix of old and new or crawl the Cahuenga Corridor where the party pups don't get started 'til long past midnight. Fly your rainbow flag on Santa Monica Blvd or look sexy by the sea at a club in Santa Monica. Tired? Relax with old-school martinis in the Polo Lounge and see who struts in next.

As for getting oriented, it's easy. A few roads run east–west across town – Sunset Blvd, Wilshire Blvd and Pico Blvd to name the big three – while the primary east–west freeway is the 10. Major north–south thoroughfares include Highway 1 (aka Lincoln Blvd and the Pacific Coast Hwy or PCH), La Cienega Blvd, Fairfax Blvd and La Brea Blvd with the 405 and the 110 being the primary north–south freeways. Got it? Then let the games begin.

# >HOLLYWOOD

America loves a comeback, and Hollywood's is long overdue. The neighborhood's rise to stardom began with a 1920s ad campaign for Hollywoodland, a residential hillside development with its name announced to the world with towering white letters. The Egyptian, the first of the grand movie palaces on Hollywood Blvd, premiered *Robin Hood* in 1922, and the glamorous boulevard was born.

But the Depression hit and glamour faded. By the 1950s, even the big white sign knew the party was over, the 'land' portion giving one last sigh before toppling over. For decades the boulevard was more grit than glitter; confused tourists wandered the courtyard at Grauman's Chinese Theatre, convinced that Hollywood was hiding just beyond Gable's concrete footprints.

The massive Hollywood & Highland shopping and entertainment complex sparked a sequel in 2001, luring back locals as well as tourists. New theaters, nightclubs and restaurants, especially near happening Cahuenga Corridor, are restoring the buzz, and condo developers have sprung into action. Box office results aren't in, but a possible blockbuster awaits.

# HOLLYWOOD

## ◉ SEE
| | | |
|---|---|---|
| Grauman's Chinese Theatre | 1 | C3 |
| Hollywood Forever Cemetery | 2 | F5 |
| Hollywood & Highland | 3 | C3 |
| Hollywood Museum | 4 | D4 |
| Walk of Fame | 5 | D3 |

## ◖ SHOP
| | | |
|---|---|---|
| Amoeba Music | 6 | E4 |
| Hollywood Book & Poster | 7 | D4 |
| Hollywood Toys & Costumes | 8 | D4 |
| Larry Edmunds Bookshop | 9 | D4 |

## ⊙ EAT
| | | |
|---|---|---|
| Cheebo | 10 | B4 |
| Hungry Cat | 11 | E4 |
| In-n-Out Burger | 12 | C4 |
| Kung Pao Kitty | 13 | D3 |
| Roscoe's House of Chicken & Waffles | 14 | F4 |
| Sanamluang Café | 15 | H4 |
| Skooby's | 16 | D4 |
| Vert | 17 | C3 |

## ⊻ DRINK
| | | |
|---|---|---|
| Boardner's | 18 | D4 |
| Bowery | 19 | E4 |
| Cat & Fiddle | 20 | D4 |
| Musso & Frank Grill | 21 | D3 |

| | | |
|---|---|---|
| Velvet Margarita | 22 | E4 |
| Zen Zoo Tea | 23 | E4 |

## ★ PLAY
| | | |
|---|---|---|
| ArcLight Cinemas | 24 | E4 |
| Arena | (see 27) | |
| Avalon | 25 | E3 |
| Catalina Bar & Grill | 26 | D4 |
| Cinespace | (see 32) | |
| Circus Disco | 27 | D5 |
| Egyptian Theatre | 28 | D4 |
| Ford Amphitheatre | 29 | D2 |
| Hollywood Bowl | 30 | C2 |
| Hotel Café | 31 | E4 |
| IO West | 32 | E4 |

Please see over for map

Ornate and ostentatious – Grauman's Chinese Theatre

# SEE

## ☉ GRAUMAN'S CHINESE THEATRE

☎ 323-464-8111; www.manntheatres.com; 6801 Hollywood Blvd; admission $8-11.25; Ⓜ Hollywood/Highland; ♿ ⚑

Stand in the footprints of silver-screen legends in the courtyard of this grand movie palace, built in 1927. Inspired by Chinese imperial architecture, the ornate decor extends from the intricate courtyard to the grand lobby, the lounges, and the massive theater itself where current releases captivate all-ages crowds.

## ☉ HOLLYWOOD FOREVER CEMETERY

☎ 323-469-1181; www.hollywoodforever.com; 6000 Santa Monica Blvd; admission free, maps $5; 🚌 MTA 4

The rock'n'roll faithful flock to the monument of guitar-playing Johnny Ramone at this Paramount-adjacent boneyard. Other residents include Hattie McDaniel, Rudolph Valentino and Cecil B DeMille. From Bugsy Siegel's mausoleum, catch the perfectly framed view of the Hollywood sign – proving Hollywood, at least here, really is forever. Watch outdoor movie screenings in the summer (www.cinespia.org).

E F G H

¹⁰

To Hollywood
Sign (1.5mi)

N Beachwood Dr

Western Canyon Dr

GRIFFITH PARK

500 m
0.3 miles

Dearborn Dr

Fern Dell Dr

²

Franklin Ave

³

Yucca St
Capitol
Records
Tower

Hollywood/
Western

Metro Red Line

eyhound
tion

N Wilton Pl

N Western Ave

N Serrano Ave

N Kingsley Dr

**Hollywood Blvd**

**Hollywood Blvd**

25

22

Hollywood/
Vine

CBS
Studios

14

15

Ivar Ave

N Vine St

N Gower St

N Bronson Ave

N Van Ness St

**W Sunset Blvd**

⁴

19

6

23

Hollywood

24

Fountain Ave

N Normandie Ave

Santa Monica Blvd

⁵

ollywood
ecreation
Center

2

Beth Olam
Memorial Park

N Cahuenga Blvd

N Vine St

El Centro Ave

2

N Oxford Ave

Lemon Grove
Recreation
Center

101

Paramount
Studios

⁶

NEIGHBORHOODS

HOLLYWOOD

### HOLLYWOOD & HIGHLAND
☎ 323-467-6412; www.hollywood andhighland.com; cnr Hollywood Blvd & Highland Ave; ⏲ 10am-10pm Mon-Sat, 10am-7pm Sun; Ⓜ Hollywood/Highland; Ⓟ ♿

With 65 shops, 26 eateries, 12 bowling lanes, six cinemas, two nightclubs and one hotel, the towering complex at one of Hollywood's busiest intersections takes one-stop shopping to the extreme. But creating the grand spectacle is a Tinseltown tradition, and the complex's courtyard – an over-the-top reproduction of a Babylonian set from DW Griffith's 1916 epic *Intolerance* – pays homage to these movie-making roots. For a hint of modern-day glamour, imagine the adjoining Kodak Theatre on Oscar day, when the boulevard is closed and the red carpet unfurled. Four-hour parking is $2 with validation.

### HOLLYWOOD MUSEUM
☎ 323-464-7776; www.theholly woodmuseum.com; 1660 N Highland Ave; adult/senior & student/under 5yr $15/12/5; ⏲ 10am-5pm Thu-Sun; Ⓜ Hollywood/Highland; ♿

Like an aging movie mogul's long-forgotten attic, the slightly musty halls of the Hollywood Museum

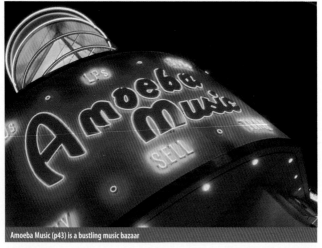
Amoeba Music (p43) is a bustling music bazaar

## BUNDLES OF FUN

Save money with LA's bundled CityPass attractions. The **Hollywood CityPass** (www.citypass .com; adult/3-11yr $49.95/39) includes admission to four Hollywood area museums and tours while the **SoCal CityPass** (adult/3-9yr $235/189) offers five attractions including Disneyland, California Adventures and Universal Studios.

are crammed with knickknacks, kitsch and some truly fascinating bits of history. From an exhibit on Marilyn Monroe's husbands to an excerpt from James Dean's homework, it's an unexpectedly fascinating mix.

### ◉ WALK OF FAME

☎ 323-469-8311; www.hollywood chamber.net; Hollywood Blvd; 🚍 MTA 2; ♿ 🚶
Marilyn Monroe? 6774 Hollywood Blvd. James Dean? 1719 Vine St. Elvis Presley? 6777 Hollywood Blvd. Nope, not last known addresses, just the exact spot for the brass star honoring these celebs on the Hollywood Walk of Fame, on Hollywood Blvd between La Brea Ave and Vine St. There are more than 2000 stars, so check the website for precise locations.

## 🛍 SHOP

### ◻ AMOEBA MUSIC Music

☎ 323-245-6400; www.amoebamusic .com; 6400 Sunset Blvd; ⏰ 10:30am-11pm Mon-Sat, 11am-9pm Sun; Ⓜ Holly-wood/Vine; Ⓟ

Grab a map at the door, then listen for the true background music at LA's beloved indie music mecca – the click, click, click of scores of customers flipping through hundreds of thousands of CDs. Oft compared to a grand music bazaar, cavernous Amoeba is a bustling community where music in all forms – CDs, DVDs, videos and vinyl – is the main commodity. Free in-house performances and substantial charitable commitments are noteworthy. Underground parking is free.

### ◻ HOLLYWOOD BOOK & POSTER

*Movie Scripts & Memorabilia*
☎ 323-465-8764; www.hollywoodbook andposter.com; 6562 Hollywood Blvd; ⏰ 11am-6pm Mon-Thu, to 7pm Fri & Sat, noon-5pm Sun; Ⓜ Hollywood/Highland
Budding screenwriters know this hardscrabble shop is the place to purchase blueprints for future success – hundreds of TV and movie scripts all for sale between $10 and $15. If you bring one they want but don't have, they'll barter. Rare movie posters and life-size Elvis cutouts also available.

## 🏠 HOLLYWOOD TOYS & COSTUMES *Costumes*

☎ 1-800-554-3444; www.hollywoodtoys .com; 6600 Hollywood Blvd; 🕙 9:30am-7pm Mon-Fri, 10am-7pm Sat, 10:30am-7pm Sun; Ⓜ Hollywood/Highland; 👤

Grab your Halloween disguise early at this gargantuan costume emporium. In front, rubber face-masks of Hillary, George and Arnold offer nonpartisan scares while top hats, swords, nurse uniforms, Jesus robes, pirate duds and lots of rubbery creepy-crawlies compete for space in the jam-packed aisles.

## 📖 LARRY EDMUNDS BOOKSHOP *Bookstore*

☎ 323-463-3273; www.larryedmunds .com; 6644 Hollywood Blvd; 🕙 10am-5:30pm; Ⓜ Hollywood/Highland

Every movie and TV book imaginable is crammed – sometimes haphazardly – onto the narrow shelves at this friendly shop that's been around for 60 years. From Kung Fu cinema to *X-Files* minutiae to the current *Creative Screenwriting*, look here first.

# 🍴 EAT

## 🍴 CHEEBO
*Healthy Californian* $-$$

☎ 323-850-7070; www.cheebo.com; 7533 W Sunset Blvd; 🕙 8am-11pm Sun-Thu, 8am-mdnight Fri & Sat; 🚌 MTA 2; Ⓥ 👤

The exterior is reminiscent of an electric cheese doodle, but the heaping salads, organic pizzas, Cuban-style sandwiches and up-beat, if quirky, waitstaff are easier on the remaining senses. The Cheebo chop salad is a favorite.

## 🍴 HUNGRY CAT
*Seafood* $$-$$$

☎ 323-462-2155; www.thehungrycat .com; 1535 N Vine St; 🕙 11:30am-2:30pm Tue-Fri, 11am-3pm Sun, 5:30pm-midnight Mon-Sat, 5-10pm Sun; Ⓜ Hollywood/Vine

Hollywood hep cats know their way to the zinc raw bar at Suzanne Goin and David Lentz' seafood hideaway – tucked behind Borders books – where peel-and-eat

---

### HAVING HANNIBAL LECTER FOR DINNER

The kitschy Hollywood Museum has one unexpected highlight – Hannibal Lecter's eerie prison cell, exactly as seen in *Silence of the Lambs*. After filming shut down, the entire set – including the prison corridor – was dismantled at Universal Studios and carried piece by piece to the museum's dark basement where it's now on display and available for renting. In fact, LA police chief William J Bratton has held two dinner parties there. As one tourist aptly inquired, 'I wonder what they served?' Fava beans and chianti, perhaps?

Dinner party destination – Hannibal Lecter's prison cell (p44) at the Hollywood Museum (p42)

shrimp, oysters on the half shell and savory fish du jour specials shine. For seafood-avoiders, the hefty Pug Burger is a must, a smoky affair memorably slathered with avocado, bacon and blue cheese.

### KUNG PAO KITTY Asian  $$
☎ 323-465-0110; 6445 Hollywood Blvd; ☽ noon-10pm Mon-Thu, noon-midnight Fri, 6pm-midnight Sat, 6-10pm Sun; 🚌 Hollywood/Highland

Fat cats and tomcats follow the pretty kitties to the late-night kitchen at this dependable Asian eatery in the heart of Hollywood. The mild, mixed-Asian menu – curries, noodles and General Tso

standards – regularly fuel the bar-hopping masses. Try the red curry or the namesake Kitty's Kung Pao.

### ROSCOE'S HOUSE OF CHICKEN & WAFFLES
*Southern*  $-$$
☎ 323-466-7453; www.roscoeschicken andwaffles.com; 1514 N Gower St; ☽ 8:30am-midnight Mon-Fri, to 4am Sat & Sun; Ⓜ Hollywood/Vine; ♿

It's not spiffy, the lighting's not so great, and the decor's best described as well worn and wooden. But for LA's best Southern soul food, look no further than this 30-year-old landmark where the namesake dish is can't-miss. The combo sounds strange but the

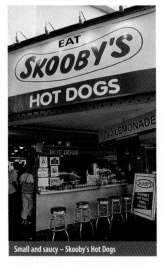

Small and saucy – Skooby's Hot Dogs

reality – crispy, juicy fried chicken with a side of soft, syrupy waffles – is simply delish. There's salad on the menu, but why?

### 🍴 SANAMLUANG CAFÉ Thai $

☎ 323-660-8006; 5176 Hollywood Blvd; 🕒 10.30am-3am; 🚌 MTA 217; Ⓟ

If the thought of dining in a tiny, rundown strip mall in Hollywood's grittier east side sounds unappealing, read no further. But if you savor the thrill of a good culinary adventure, grab your keys for a trip to Thai Town for some of the best noodles around. The no-frills, pictures-of-the-food decor may

be uninspiring, but all is forgiven once that huge, simmering bowl of General's Noodles – stuffed to the rim with shrimp, duck and barbecued pork – arrives at your table. Pad thai is available for beginners. Cash only and open late.

### 🍴 SKOOBY'S Hot Dogs $

☎ 323-468-3647; www.skoobys.com; 6654 Hollywood Blvd; 🕒 11am-midnight; Ⓜ Hollywood/Highland; ♿

Hot dogs are king at this pocket-sized paean to America's favorite guilty pleasure. Grab a seat at the Walk-of-Fame-adjacent counter and order a 7-inch dog with Guinness chili, grilled onions and peppers, or keep it easy-squeezy with a squirt of spicy mustard. Fries and dipping sauce are scrumptious. Cash only.

### 🍴 VERT Fusion $$$

☎ 323-491-1300; www.wolfgangpuck.com; 6801 Hollywood Blvd, 4th fl; 🕒 11:30am-10pm Mon-Fri, noon-10pm Sat & Sun; Ⓜ Hollywood/Vine; Ⓟ ♿

The exquisite, almost too-pretty-to-eat salads are the must-try dishes at Wolfgang Puck's stylish new addition to the Hollywood & Highland complex. While you wait for your leafy lunch, sip on a signature Bellini (prosecco and green apple juice) and watch the continuous parade of passersby – the adjoining exterior walkway provides an awesome view of the

**SECRET MENUS**

Shhh... LA's best burger chain has a secret menu known only to locals. And now you. **In-n-Out Burger** (7009 Sunset Blvd; www.inandout.com) is a true LA phenom, as the cars jamming the drive-thru can attest. Burgers, fries, soda, shakes – that's all it offers under the yellow-and-red roof but fresh and simple works, as does the burgers' tasty sauce. The secret menu adds a twist to the preparation. Order your burger Animal Style for an awesome grilled onion topping, Protein Style for no bun, or, if you're hungry – the 4 by 4.

Hollywood sign. Parking costs $2 per hour with validation.

# DRINK

## ☿ BOARDNER'S *Bar*

☎ 323-462-9621; www.boardners.com; 1652 N Cherokee Ave; Ⓜ Hollywood/Highland

Keeping barflies boozy since 1942, this dimly lit dive is hot once again with the hipsters – just ask the old salt keeping track from his barside perch. For celeb hounds, Kiefer Southerland, Heath Ledger and Vince Vaughn have been spotted here. The B52 nightclub in back draws a different crowd – Saturday night's Bar Sinister admits only those in black or fetish-appropriate attire.

## ☿ BOWERY *Gastropub*

☎ 323-465-3400; www.thebowery hollywood.com; 6268 Sunset Blvd; ☽ noon-2am Mon-Fri, 6pm-2am Sat & Sun; 🚌 MTA 2

It may be new, but this nocturnal New York–style pub is the bar

of choice for bartenders and waitstaff looking for a late-night toddy. It's small, so arrive early for a table. Some swear the burger, cooked just as requested, is a life-changing experience. The cast of *Heroes* occasionally drops by for lunch.

## ☿ CAT & FIDDLE *British Pub*

☎ 323-468-3800; www.thecatandfiddle .com; 6530 Sunset Blvd; ☽ 11am-2am; 🚌 MTA 2

From Morrissey to Frodo, you never know who might be sipping Guinness on the leafy, laid-back courtyard patio where it's more about friends and conversation than faux-hawks and working the deal.

## ☿ MUSSO & FRANK GRILL *Cocktails*

☎ 323-467-7788; 6667 Hollywood Blvd; ☽ 11am-11pm Tue-Sat; Ⓜ Hollywood/Highland

History and martinis are the draw nowadays at this red-boothed landmark that's been serving up drinks to writers, actors and rockers for the better part of a century. For a noirish night out, order a no-frills martini at the dark wooden bar and soak up the boozy spirits of Chandler, Fitzgerald and Hammett.

### ▼ VELVET MARGARITA
*Mexican Cantina*

☎ 323-469-2000; www.velvetmargarita.com; 1612 N Cahuenga Blvd; ⏱ 11am-2am Mon-Thu, 11am-4am Fri, 6pm-4am Sat, 6pm-2am Sun; Ⓜ Hollywood/Vine

Elvis lives at the Velvet Margarita. And so do hordes of party hounds, all swilling $10 margaritas in a dark palace of King-inspired kitsch. Sombreros, velvet Elvises, dancing skeletons and cheesy B-movies on the wall – it's Day-of-the-Dead meets Graceland.

### ▼ ZEN ZOO TEA *Tea*

☎ 323-962-9969; www.zenzootea.com; 1517 N Vine St; ⏱ 9am-10pm Mon-Thu, 9am-11pm Fri, 10am-11pm Sat, 10am-9pm Sun; 🚌 MTA 2; ♿

A frothy alternative to coffee, Zen Zoo's tonic-infused teas inspire alertness, confidence and optimism – and that's just from reading the menu. No matter which flavorful Zenfusion you select – green tea, black tea, yerba mate – make sure to include the pearl tapioca 'boba' balls.

## ★ PLAY

### ★ ARCLIGHT CINEMAS *Cinema*

☎ 323-464-4226; www.arclightcinemas.com; 6360 W Sunset Blvd; adult Fri & Sat after 6pm & Sun before 6pm $14 , all other times $11, 2-12yr before/after 6pm $7.75/9.75; 🚌 MTA 2; ♿ ♿

Preselected seats, an in-house bar and friendly employees – plus proximity to Amoeba Music – make this relative newcomer one of the primo theaters in LA. Star-sighting potential is also exceptionally high, though you won't see Quentin Tarantino, who's opposed to the strict 'No entry after the movie starts' policy. He has a point – everyone *is* running late in LA.

### ★ AVALON *Nightclub*

☎ 323-462-8900; www.avalonhollywood.com; 1735 N Vine St; admission $20-35; Ⓜ Hollywood/Vine

Now booking superstar DJs for its Saturday-night electronic dance

> ### JOLLY ON THE TROLLEY
> Thursday through Saturday nights, the Holly Trolley loops past bars, restaurants and clubs on Hollywood Blvd and Sunset Ave from Highland Ave east to Vine. The trolley – more a reconfigured bus – runs every 15 minutes from 6:30pm to 2:30am, and the fare is $1. See www.ladottransit.com/other/trolley for a map.

Cinema-turns-club at Cinespace

scene 'Avaland,' the 1400-capacity club hopes to win the battle of the Saturday-night dance clubs. Weekly, the cavernous venue introduces live bands and local DJs into mix. With its late-night permit, you'll see Avalon party kids spilling onto the sidewalk as the sun comes up.

### ✪ CATALINA BAR & GRILL
*Jazz Club*

☎ 323-466-2210; www.catalinajazzclub
.com; 6725 W Sunset Blvd; Ⓜ Hollywood/
Highland

The exterior of LA's smoothest jazz club looks more like an office complex than a sexy club, but once inside the spacious but sultry digs,

all is forgiven. Dizzy Gillespie, Art Blakely and the Marsalis brothers have graced the stage but up-and-comers are spotlighted too.

### ✪ CINESPACE *Cinema*

☎ 323-817-3456; www.cinespace.info;
6356 Hollywood Blvd; movie included
with main meal; Ⓨ 6pm-2am Thu-Sat;
Ⓜ Hollywood/Vine

Thursday through Saturday, it's dinner-and-date night at easygoing Cinespace, where classic movies and cutting-edge indies are screened for crowds wanting more than a trough of buttery popcorn. After the show, the theater morphs into a sexy, but not-hipper-than-thou, nightclub.

Shows and stunning scenery at the Hollywood Bowl

### ⭐ CIRCUS DISCO *Dance Club*
☎ 323-462-1291; www.circusdisco.com; 6655 Santa Monica Blvd; admission up to $30; 🚌 MTA 156

It's a seven-ring circus Saturday nights when DJs spin house, trance, hip-hop, and '80s music in seven separate rooms in Circus' 40,000-sq-ft warehouse. Crowds swarm the laser-filled dance floors for a multilingual, multithemed DJ-powered bacchanalia. On Tuesdays it's

boys night for guys who like guys, and next door at gay-slanted **Arena** ( ☎ 323-462-0714; www.arenanightclub.com), it's boys night a lot more often.

### ⭐ EGYPTIAN THEATRE *Cinema*
☎ 323-466-3456; www.egyptian theatre.com; 6712 Hollywood Blvd; adult/senior & student $10/8; 🕙 Wed-Sun; Ⓜ Hollywood/Highland; ♿

With a design inspired by the discovery of King Tut's tomb, the

Egyptian held Hollywood's first star-studded premiere in 1922 – Douglas Fairbanks' *Robin Hood*. Today, moviegoers settle in for tributes, retrospectives and post-screening Q&As with directors, screenwriters and actors.

### ⭐ FORD AMPHITHEATRE
*Outdoor Concerts*
☎ 323-461-3673; www.fordamphitheatre.com; 2580 Cahuenga Blvd E; admission $5-45; 🚌 163; 👶
Every seat is within 100ft of the stage at this up-close-and-personal outdoor amphitheater. With the Hollywood Hills as a back-drop, catch indie bands, foreign movies and dance troupes from May to October. Picnics welcome.

### ⭐ HOLLYWOOD BOWL
*Outdoor Concerts*
☎ 323-850-2000; www.hollywoodbowl.com; 2301 N Highland Ave; admission from $1; 🕐 late Jun-late Sep; Ⓜ Hollywood/Highland; 👶
The largest natural outdoor amphitheater in the US, the beloved Bowl stages symphonies under the stars, *Sound of Music* singalongs and perfect-for-chillin'-outside faves like Lyle Lovett and Sheryl Crow. Now the summer home of the LA Phil, it also hosts big-name rock, jazz

and blues acts. Wine-and-cheese picnics are a popular preshow tradition.

### ⭐ HOTEL CAFÉ *Live Music*
☎ 323-461-2040; www.hotelcafe.com; 1623½ N Cahuenga Blvd; admission $10-12; 🕐 shows nightly; Ⓜ Hollywood/Vine
Unsigned bands get their due at charmingly intimate Hotel Café, where an appreciative crowd comes for the music and not the scene. Seen as a stepping-stone for up-and-comers, the calendar includes an eclectic mix – from touring Australian cult faves John Butler Trio to rock legends such as Pete Townsend. The narrow, red-brick interior fills quick, so arrive early for a table or a meal.

### ⭐ IO WEST *Improv*
☎ 323-962-7560; www.iowest.com; 6366 Hollywood Blvd; admission $5-10; Ⓜ Hollywood/Vine
Toss out the phrase 'giant mushroom' and watch the cast spin a 45-minute skit. Long form is the specialty at this cozy corner theater – the LA branch of Olympic Improv Chicago – where you might catch familiar faces from *The Office* or *SNL* honing their comedy chops. Cocktails served.

# >GRIFFITH PARK, LOS FELIZ & SILVER LAKE

Griffith Park is LA's own personal country club. A Christmas gift to the city from mining mogul Griffith J Griffith in 1896, the 4210-acre park boasts golf courses, tennis courts, bridle trails, a classic carousel, a miniature passenger train, a rowdy zoo and 53 miles of hiking paths – one of them leading to Batman's very own batcaves. Those hungry for more intellectual diversions can wander the cowboy culture exhibits at the Museum of the American West, study the stars in Griffith Observatory's revamped planetarium, or enjoy an outdoor concert and picnic at the Greek Theatre. Be aware that the view may look a bit scorched in places: a fire in May 2007 charred 817 acres.

A bit of the park's wild spirit rubs off on Los Feliz and Silver Lake denizens living in its hilly shadows. Los Feliz is home to its fair share of up-and-coming artists, actors and writers, while Silver Lake is known for its laid-back, low-key gay scene. The boho-chic inhabitants of both neighborhoods keep cafés, bookstores and vintage shops abuzz with late-night energy and liberal attitudes.

## GRIFFITH PARK, LOS FELIZ & SILVER LAKE

### ⊙ SEE
Griffith Observatory ......1 C2
Griffith Park Ranger
Station ...........................2 B3
Hollyhock House ...........3 B4
LA Zoo & Botanical
Gardens ........................4 B1
Museum of the
American West...............5 C1

### ◻ SHOP
Oou .............................6 B4
Skylight Books .............7 B4

Squaresville..................(see 7)
Sunset Junction............8 C5
Wacko...........................9 B4

### 🍴 EAT
Blair's.........................10 D4
Café at the End of
the Universe ...............(see 2)
El Conquistador...........11 C5
Fred 62 .......................12 B4
Gingergrass ................13 D4
Square One Dining .....14 B5
Yuca's.........................15 C4

### ⓨ DRINK
Bigfoot Lodge .............16 D3
Edendale Grill Mixville
Bar .............................17 D4
Good Luck Bar ............18 C4

### ★ PLAY
Greek Theatre..............19 B3
Little Temple ...............20 C5

# SEE

## GRIFFITH OBSERVATORY

☎ 213-473-0800; www.griffith observatory.org; 2800 E Observatory Rd; admission free, shuttle adult/senior & 5-12yr/under 5yr $8/4/free; ⊙ noon-10pm Tue-Fri, 10am-10pm Sat & Sun; ⓚ

With an additional 40,000 sq ft, a new multilevel exhibit gallery, a 200-seat theater, 60 new exhibits, a café and a giftstore, the new observatory in Griffith Park is ready for the masses. But for now, it's by timed-entry reservation only. Made by phone or email, res-

ervations provide a set entry time and guaranteed shuttle seat. No drive-up access is currently permitted, but stargazers can access observatory shuttles from various locations. And yes, it's worth the hassle. See also p19.

## GRIFFITH PARK

☎ 323-913-4688; www.lacity.org/rap; 4730 Crystal Springs Dr; admission free; ⊙ 6am-10pm, hiking & bridle paths until sunset; 🚌 MTA 96; Ⓟ ⓚ

SoCal naturalist John Muir once said the clearest way into the universe is through forest wilder-

Rich eccentric + stubborn genius = Hollyhock House

## OFF THE BEATEN PATH

Instead of jogging to nowhere in the hotel gym, zip up a short, easy-to-access mountain trail for amazing views and a dose of California sunshine, smog regardless. For canyons and oceans, try the 3-mile Temescal Canyon trail at Temescal Gateway Park (www.lamountains .com) off Sunset Blvd in Pacific Palisades. The payoff at Will Rogers State Park (www.park .ca.gov) is a possible polo match played at the base of the 2-mile Inspiration Point trail. For celeb sightings as well as city views, there's no better ramble than Hollywood's Runyon Canyon (www.laparks.org) at the end of Fuller Ave.

Fires ripped across Griffith Park in May 2007, leaving the Charlie Turner Trail to Mt Hollywood – one of the finest viewpoints in the city – looking like a lunar landscape. Call the ranger station at ☎ 323-913-4888 for the latest trail conditions.

ness. The tree-covered acres at sprawling Griffith Park – the country's biggest city park with urban wilderness – proves his point with miles of trails and a seemingly endless supply of stunning views. Stop by the ranger's office for a map and list of attractions.

### ◉ HOLLYHOCK HOUSE
☎ 323-644-6269; www.hollyhockhouse .net; Barnsdall Art Park, 4800 Hollywood Blvd, Los Feliz; adult/senior & student/ under 12yr $7/3/free; ⊙ tours hourly 12:30-3:30pm Wed-Sun; Ⓜ Vermont/ Sunset; Ⓟ

Oil heiress Aline Barnsdall commissioned Frank Lloyd Wright to design this hilltop home in 1919. As happens with rich eccentrics and stubborn geniuses, the project ended sourly and was finished by architect Rudolph Schindler. Due to Wright's Romanza-style design there's an

easy flow between rooms and courtyards. Note abstract imagery of the hollyhock, Aline's preferred flower, throughout.

### ◉ LA ZOO & BOTANICAL GARDENS
☎ 323-644-4200; www.lazoo.org; 5333 Zoo Dr, Griffith Park; adult/senior/2-12yr/ under 2yr $10/7/5/free; ⊙ 10am-5pm; 🚌 MTA 96; Ⓟ ⓖ ♿

Meerkats are the current squeezables of the Disney set, and one well-placed, big-eyed Timon wows kids entering the zoo. From there, undisputed crowdpleasers include swinging gibbons, frolicking sea lions, posturing chimpanzees, cuddling koalas and, according to the zoo's director, anything currently defecating. The zoo is deceptively larger than it appears from outside; you'll need at least 2½ hours. New gorilla and elephant reserves coming soon.

Cowboys ride again at the Museum of the American West

### MUSEUM OF THE AMERICAN WEST

☎ 323-667-2000; www.autrynational center.org; 4700 Western Heritage Way, Griffith Park; adult/senior & student/3-12yr/under 3yr $9/5/3/free, free 2nd Tue of month; ⏰ 10am-5pm Tue-Sun; 🚌 MTA 96; ℗ ♿ ⛲

Unabashed exhibits on the good, the bad and the violent during America's westward expansion rope in even the most reluctant of cowpokes. Annie Oakley's shotgun, a Concord stagecoach ('It don't break down, it only wears out') and Wyatt Earp's handwritten notes on the gunfight at the OK Corral are among the many treasures scat-tered throughout the museum's six themed galleries. And of course, a museum endowed by Gene Autry isn't complete without one of the singing cowboy's guitars.

## 🛍 SHOP

### OOU *Fashion*

☎ 323-665-6263; 1764 N Vermont Ave, Los Feliz; ⏰ noon-7pm Mon-Sat, to 6pm Sun; 🚌 MTA 204, 754

Hip, trendy, with a dash of funky attitude, this compact but well-stocked boutique – with a focus on young designers – has jackets, tees and boots that keep the Los Feliz fashion-forward safely ahead of the curve.

## 🏠 SKYLIGHT BOOKS *Books*

☎ 323-660-1175; www.skylightbooks
.com; 1818 N Vermont Ave, Los Feliz;
🕐 10am-10pm; 🚌 MTA 204, 754

If bookstores were judged on the
quality of resident cats, indie Skylight Books would win paws down.
Fortunately, Skylight's fiction, po-
etry and California travel sections
are just as noteworthy as lurking
feline Lucy. Exposed brick walls,
a willowy tree and nameworthy
skylight add to the friendly vibe.

## 🏠 SQUARESVILLE
*Vintage Clothing*

☎ 323-669-8464; 1800 N Vermont Ave;
🕐 11am-8pm Tue-Sat, noon-7pm Sun &
Mon; 🚌 MTA204, 754

Square never felt so right at this
two-story corner shop jam-packed
with gently used – but oh-so-
happenin' – T-shirts, jeans, dresses
and accessories. Upstairs you'll
find men's and shoes. It buys, sells
and trades.

## 🏠 WACKO *Gifts*

☎ 323-663-0122; 4633 Hollywood Blvd,
Los Feliz; 🕐 11am-7pm Mon-Wed,
11am-9pm Thu-Sat, noon- 6pm Sun;
🚌 MTA 26

There's a present for every member of your dysfunctional circle
at this eclectic, bursting-with-
kitsch, garishly painted giftorium:
dashboard Jesuses, tiki statues,
soap plant candles, and tomes on

## SUNSET JUNCTION

For indie-minded shopping, check out
Silver Lake's funky but fashionable
Sunset Junction at the intersection of
Sunset and Santa Monica Blvds. It's
a happily-not-hip little corner where
sassy sundresses, one-of-a-kind kicks,
local coffee, worldwide cheeses and
low-key patio dining draw a laid-back
neighborhood crowd. Worth a stop are
the **Cheese Store of Silver Lake** (3926
W Sunset Blvd), **Casbah Café** (3900 W
Sunset Blvd) and **Undefeated** (3827
W Sunset Blvd). The massive Sunset
Junction Street Fair draws multicultural
crowds for bands, food and community
mingling in late August.

cult cinema. Staff loiter liked bored
British rockers but a fun Elvis
section makes up for perceived
indifference. For a low-culture
immersion, wander back to the La
Luz de Jesus gallery and its intrigu-
ing array of edgy, post-pop art.

## 🍴 EAT

### 🍴 BLAIR'S *American* $$-$$$

☎ 323-660-1882; 2903 Rowena Ave,
Silver Lake; 🕐 7am-10pm Mon-Thu, to
11pm Sat & Sun; 🚌 MTA 201

Chef Marshall Blair, formerly of
downtown's Water Grill (p133), de-
livers upscale comfort food to an
appreciative local crowd. Despite
the haphazard service and a too-
dark interior, Blair's divine seafood

## Juana Veliz
*LatinoLA.com contributor, Latino market spinmaster and PR guru*

**Best places to check out Latino culture in LA?** Plazita Olvera (p128) is the birthplace of Los Angeles. It's a plaza with restaurants, crafts, dancing, mariachis, and there's a great mural by Mexican artist David Sisqueiros. **How about less-touristy areas?** Heading east, Cesar Chavez Ave will take you into East LA. Go right on Boyle Ave and left on 1st St and you'll hit Boyle Heights...at Mariachi Plaza you'll get serenaded. Really, in a city where Latinos represent 47% of the population, you don't have to look too far. **Best salsa dancing?** Salserosweb.com has the latest on clubs and events, but I love El Floridita in Hollywood on Monday nights. Actually, anywhere Johnny Polanco plays. **How about the other salsa?** The chips and salsa are to die for at El Compadre (p61), on Sunset near Dodger Stadium. **Who mixes the best margarita?** Velvet Margarita (p48). They have actual velvet throughout...and great Latino-inspired pieces like the calacas (skeletons). They show black-and-white Cantinaflas films in the background. **Favorite coffee shop?** Antigua Cultural Coffee House (p134) is homey and family oriented. I like the vibe and the coffee.

and beef dishes have vaulted this low-key corner restaurant to the top of many locals' fave list. Crab cakes and short ribs – yummo! Reservations recommended.

### 🍴 CAFÉ AT THE END OF THE UNIVERSE *American*                              $

**www.griffithobservatory.org/vcafe.html; 2800 E Observatory Rd, Griffith Observatory;** 🕐 **noon-9pm Tue-Fri, 10am-9pm Sat & Sun; observatory shuttle;** ♿
Wolfgang Puck's latest satellite venture – a cafeteria-style café – orbits just past the observatory's Cosmic Connection hallway. Designed with retro space-age flair, the café offers tasty gourmet sandwiches, soups and salads. Grab a turkey and cranberry sandwich then hit the patio for inspiring views of the Hollywood sign. (See also p19.)

### 🍴 EL CONQUISTADOR *Mexican*                              $$

☎ **323-666-5136; 3701 W Sunset Blvd, Silver Lake;** 🕐 **4-10pm Mon, 11am-10pm Tue-Thu & Sun, 11am-11pm Fri & Sat;** 🚌 **MTA 2, 4;** ♿
In a garden setting straight out of a Mexican fishing village, this bustling respite serves traditional regional dishes including Sonorese chicken and mole. Unrestrained pastels and Easter-bunny decor complement the strong margaritas. Or vice versa.

### 🍴 FRED 62 *Diner*                              $

☎ **323-667-0062; www.fred62.com; 1850 N Vermont Ave;** 🕐 **24hr;** 🚌 **MTA 204, 754;** ♿
It's orange, it's retro, it's a little ironic, and it's also open all night. The grub's standard diner fare – omelets, pancakes – but named with funky flair and given the occasional twist. Budding Elvises hanker for the Hunka Hunka Burnin' Love pancakes with peanut butter, chocolate chips and bananas.

### 🍴 GINGERGRASS *Vietnamese*                              $-$$

☎ **323-644-1600; www.gingergrass .com; 2396 Glendale Blvd, Silver Lake;** 🕐 **11:30am-3pm daily, 5-10pm Sun-Thu, 5-10:30pm Fri & Sat;** 🚌 **MTA 92;** 🅿
Lemongrass chicken, noodle bowls and vegetarian *pho* – fresh, light, and prepared with gently flavored care at this always bustling local's haven. Best of all? It's an easy drive down Riverside from Griffith Park.

### 🍴 SQUARE ONE DINING *Breakfast*                              $-$$

☎ **323-661-1109; www.squareone dining.com; 4854 Fountain Ave, Los Feliz;** 🕐 **8am-4pm;** 🚌 **MTA 175**
Breakfasts here are so darn good you'll want to lick your square white plate. The decor's not much but thick slabs of bacon, fluffy egg

Log-cabin comfort at Bigfoot Lodge

dishes and unbleached heirloom grits confirm the focus is where it should be. Artists, couples and business brunchers fill tables for the all-organic menu, but for a different view, grab a window seat and watch the buttoned-down faithful at the nearby Scientology complex.

### YUCA'S *Mexican* $
☎ 323-662-1214; 2056 Hillhurst Ave; 🕙 11am-6pm Mon-Sat; 🚌 MTA 204, 754; 👶
They may have paved paradise and put up a taco hut but who's complaining? At Yuca's tiny taco shack, tucked between a liquor store and nail salon, they've served fast, hot, authentic tacos for years. Some say they're the best in town. Place your order at the counter and see for yourself – won't cost ya more than four bucks.

# DRINK
### BIGFOOT LODGE *Bar*
☎ 323-662-9227; www.bigfootlodge .com; 3172 Los Feliz Blvd, Los Feliz; 🕙 5pm-2am; 🚌 MTA 180, 181
Smokey the Bear presides over this laid-back log-cabin setting, a cool spot to camp out for a drink or two (try the minty Girl Scout cookie). The action heats up Tuesday for ladies night and Wednesday for Club London Calling.

### EDENDALE GRILL MIXVILLE BAR *Bar*
☎ 323-666-2000; www.edendalegrill .com; 2838 Rowena Ave; 🕙 5pm-midnight Sun-Wed, to 2am Thu-Sat; 🚌 MTA 92
Gay, straight, 20s, 30s and Hollywood refugees – it's a five-alarm crowd on weekends at this former Silver Lake firestation. The mahogany bar, pressed-in ceiling and wide bay doors lend a certain old-school gravitas to the nonstop,

late-night reveling. Locals fill the bar and patios weeknights.

## ▼ EL COMPADRE
*Mexican Cantina*

☎ 3213-250-4505; 1449 W Sunset Blvd, Echo Park; ⏰ 11am-1:30pm Sun-Thu, 11:30am-1:30am Fri & Sat

Excuse me, waiter? It seems my margarita is on fire. It's supposed to be? Slurp. Mmmm. Can I have another? If you've never had a flaming margarita, order up and enjoy, with addictive chips and salsa at Echo Park's liveliest cantina. Open late, its U-shaped booths and festive decor are perfect for rowdy groups. If this downtown-adjacent location isn't convenient, check out the **Hollywood branch** (7408 W Hollywood Blvd).

## ▼ GOOD LUCK BAR *Bar*

☎ 323-666-3524; 1514 Hillhurst Ave; ⏰ 7pm-2am Mon-Thu, 8pm-2am Fri & Sat; 🚌 MTA 2

### TROUBLE IN PARADISE?

A 2005 city master plan for Griffith Park has raised hackles with its development goals – aerial trams, a culinary school, a hotel and multilevel parking garages – that some fear will turn this natural oasis into a mini-Disneyland. Opposition forces are gearing for a fight. Visit http://savegriffithpark.org for more details on the controversy and a link to the master plan.

It's decked out like a fantasy Chinese opium den, and the paper lanterns at this cultish watering hole cast a siren's red glow. The clientele is cool, the jukebox is loud, and the drinks are seductively strong. Be sure to pick up a matchbook.

## ★ PLAY

## ★ GREEK THEATRE
*Performing Arts*

☎ 323-665-5857; www.greektheatrela.com; 2700 N Vermont Ave, Griffith Park; ⏰ early May–mid-Oct; 🚌 MTA 180, 181

Appreciative summer crowds love the vibe and the variety – Lyle Lovett, Tina Turner, the Russian Ballet, Death Cab for Cutie, Gipsy Kings – at this 5800-seat outdoor venue tucked in the woodsy hills of Griffith Park. Be forewarned, parking is stacked, so plan on a post-show wait.

## ★ LITTLE TEMPLE *Nightclub*

☎ 323-660-4540; www.littletemple.com; 4519 Santa Monica Blvd, Silver Lake; ⏰ 9pm-2am Tue-Sun; Ⓜ Vermont/Santa Monica

Afro-Cuban, deep house, hip-hop and a side of salsa keep this groovin' Little Temple swelling with happy hipsters. A sexy spin-off from its Santa Monica sister, this Asian-themed club with a red lantern glow keeps things loose with beat-driven DJs.

# >WEST HOLLYWOOD

From the welcoming rainbow flags on Santa Monica Blvd to the chattering masses at the ever-expanding Abbey to the over-the-top exuberance of the Halloween Carnaval, West Hollywood might give Disneyland a run as the happiest place on earth.

How did West Hollywood become the center of so much fun? For one thing, the 1.9-sq-mile neighborhood remained unincorporated for most of the 20th century, its lax governmental oversight allowing for an easy flow of liquor during Prohibition. This freewheeling spirit infused future attitudes and can be seen today in the rock'n'roll party scene of Sunset Strip, in the gay-fueled weekend fun of Santa Monica Blvd, and in the cutting-edge attitude of the Pacific Design Center and surrounding Avenues of Arts & Design. As for attitude, every celebutante worth her tabloid cover has plenty to throw around in these parts; just peek into the boutiques lining Robertson Blvd for a glimpse. But take a longer look at intersections – some of these starlets don't drive very well. And the 6000 Russian immigrants living here? They take it all in stride.

## WEST HOLLYWOOD

### ◉ SEE
Museum of Contempory
Art ..........................1  B3
Pacific Design Center .....2  B3

### 🏠 SHOP
Bodhi Tree .....................3  C3
Book Soup ......................4  B2
Fred Segal ......................5  D3
Kitson ...........................6  B4
Lisa Kline ......................7  B4

### 🍴 EAT
Boule .............................8  C3
Chaya Brasserie ............9  B4
Dan Tana's ...................10  B3
Griddle Café.................11  D1
Koi ...............................12  C3
O-Bar ..........................13  D2
Sweet Lady Jane..........14  D3

### 🍸 DRINK
Abbey ..........................15  B3
Elixr Tonics & Teas.......16  C3
Formosa Café ..............17  F2

Here..............................18  B3
Jones ............................19  F2
Skybar ..........................20  C1
Urth Caffé.....................21  C3

### ⭐ PLAY
House of Blues..............22  C1
Key Club........................23  B2
Rage .............................24  B2
Roxy..............................25  B2
Troubadour...................26  B3
Whisky-a-Go-Go ..........27  B2

V

NEIGHBORHOODS

WEST HOLLYWOOD

# SEE

## PACIFIC DESIGN CENTER

☎ 310-657-0800; www.pacificdesign center.com; 8687 Melrose Ave; 🕙 9am-5pm Mon-Fri; 🚌 10, 11

The blue and green leviathan at the corner of Melrose and San Vicente – the 'Blue Whale' – is a perfect launchpad for exploring the nearby Avenues of Arts & Design. Inside, more than 130 showrooms highlight furniture, fabrics and architectural products of interest to design professionals. The **Museum of Contemporary Art** (MOCA; ☎ 310-289-5223) maintains a satellite gallery here with rotating design- and architecture-related exhibits.

# SHOP

## BODHI TREE *Bookstore*

☎ 310-659-1733; www.bodhitree.com; 8585 Melrose Ave; 🕙 new bookstore 10am-11pm, used bookstore to 7pm; 🚌 MTA 10, 11

Here since 1970, this cosy cottage of enlightenment carries an impressively broad range of spiritual-minded books – Buddhism, Christianity, astrology, shamanism – that's attractive to students and dabblers alike. Psychic readings offered daily.

## BOOK SOUP *Bookstore*

☎ 310-659-3110; www.booksoup .com; 8818 Sunset Blvd; 🕙 9am-9pm

Cutting-edge Pacific Design Center

Mon-Sun, newsstand 9am-6pm Mon-Fri, 10am-6pm Sat & Sun; 🚍 MTA 2; Ⓟ
Like a favorite lit-professor's office, this bibliophile's gem is jam-packed floor to ceiling with hardbacks, paperbacks and everything in between. Art, film and California travel are especially strong at this indie landmark in the heart of Sunset Strip. Author appearances range from Ron Jeremy to David Mamet.

### 🛍 FRED SEGAL *Boutique*
☎ 323-651-4129; 8100 Melrose Ave; ⏱ 10am-7pm Mon-Sat, noon-6pm Sun; 🚍 MTA 10, 11; Ⓟ
This ivy-covered icon is really several high-end boutiques clustered under one impossibly chic but slightly snooty roof. Celebs circle for the latest from Jet, Jill Stewart and McQ, while those in the know (including savvy stars) arrive early for deep discounts at the September sale. Café and salon onsite. There's also a store in **Santa Monica** (Map pp96–7, C3; ☎ 310-458-9940; 500 Broadway).

### 🛍 KITSON *Women's Clothing*
☎ 310-859-2652; www.shopkitson.com; 115 S Robertson Blvd; ⏱ 10am-7pm Mon-Fri, 9am-7:30pm Sat, 11am-6pm Sun; 🚍 MTA 220
Follow the fun, funky and fab to this green-and-white pop tart where moneyed sceney-boppers flock for up-to-the-second fashion. High-energy tunes will keep you

flipping fast through hoodies, purses, shoes, and stacks and stacks of denim. For fashion-forward families there's also **Kitson Men** (146 N Robertson) and **Kitson Kids** (108 S Robertson Blvd).

### 🛍 LISA KLINE
*Women's Clothing*
☎ 310-246-0907; www.lisakline.com; 136 S Robertson Blvd; ⏱ 11am-7pm Mon-Sat, noon-6pm Sun; 🚍 MTA 220
Less hectic than Kitson, Lisa Kline offers bright cheery digs, friendly service and casual couture that has kept flip-flop fashionistas and the Hollywood elite looking fab for more than a decade. See also **Lisa Kline Men** (143 S Robertson Blvd) and **Lisa Kline Kids** (123 S Robertson Blvd).

## 🍴 EAT

### 🍴 BOULE *Bakery*                                $
☎ 310-289-9977; www.boulela.com; 420 N La Cienega; ⏱ 10am-7pm Mon-Sat, noon-6pm Sun; 🚍 MTA 705
A colorful platoon of macaroons first catches the eye at this impossibly precious patisserie. Wood-accented azure walls – lined neatly with specialty oils, teapots and accessories – tower over a dazzling array of tortes, chocolates and sorbets. Simultaneously sleek, homey and over-the-top, Boule is best described as Willy Wonka meets Bree Van de Camp. These decadent delicacies are undeniably delish.

### 🍽 CHAYA BRASSERIE
*French-Japanese*          $$-$$$

☎ 310-859-8833; www.thechaya.com;
8741 Alden Dr; ⏰ 11:30am-2:30pm
Mon-Fri, 6-10:30pm Mon-Thu, 6-11pm Fri
& Sat, 6-10pm Sun; 🚌 MTA 220

Wood beams and soaring bamboo complement a spacious Asian-style atrium where Chef Shigefumi Tachibe whips up savory French dishes with Japanese flair. Savvy shoppers flock here from Robertson Blvd for great happy-hour deals on sushi and martinis. For the same great deals and taste at the beach, try sister restaurant **Chaya Venice** (Map p109, A2; 110 Navy St) on the border of Santa Monica and Venice.

### 🍽 DAN TANA'S *Italian*          $$$

☎ 310-275-9444; www.dantanas restaurant.com; 9071 Santa Monica Blvd; ⏰ 5pm-1:30am; 🚌 MTA 4

---

### ROCKING ON THE STRIP

Pining for the days when rock'n'roll sprang from passion, not primetime? Baby, Sunset Strip is calling your name. From **Whisky-a-Go-Go** (www.whiskyagogo .com; 8901 W Sunset Blvd), where The Doors were the house band, to 30-year stalwart the **Roxy** (www.theroxyonsun set.com; 9009 W Sunset Blvd) to the state-of-the-art **Key Club** ( ☎ 310-786-1712; 9039 Sunset Blvd), the Strip still rocks late night, though it skews to local bands with occasional legendary drop-bys.

---

Tightly packed booths, red-jacketed staff, smooth-as-silk cocktails and no-frills pasta – old Hollywood still lingers at Dan Tana's, open since 1964. Some say the pasta dishes are overpriced, but Jessica Alba, George Clooney and the rest of the new Hollywood crowd don't seem to mind. The caesar salad is especially good, and perfect for splitting.

### 🍽 GRIDDLE CAFÉ
*Breakfast*          $-$$

☎ 323-874-0377; www.thegriddlecafe .com; 7916 Sunset Blvd; ⏰ 7am-4pm Mon-Fri, 8am-4pm Sat & Sun; 🚌 MTA 2; Ⓥ ♿

Giant portions, friendly service and French press coffee keep the wooden tables and U-shaped counter full all morning at this tasty breakfast joint favored by Hollywood's young and tousled. Located just east of the dark-towered Directors Guild; look for the mobs huddled outside on weekend mornings. Arrive early.

### 🍽 KOI *Japanese*          $$$$

☎ 310-659-9449; 730 N La Cienega Blvd; ⏰ 6-11pm Mon-Wed, to 11:30pm Thu, to midnight Fri & Sat, to 10pm Sun; 🚌 MTA 220

Some come for celeb-spotting, some come for superior service, but all come for the spicy tuna on crispy rice at this bamboo-fortified sanctum in the heart of the TMZ. Nobodies nibble Japanese specialties in the warm, Asian-accented central dining room while patio-dwellers – Owen Wilson, David Spade, Nicolette Sheridan and Avril Lavigne – float past. Reservations recommended.

### 🍴 O-BAR American $$$
☎ 323-822-3300; www.obarrestaurant.com; 8279 Santa Monica Blvd; ⏰ 6pm-midnight Sun & Mon, to 1am Tue & Wed, to 2am Thu-Sat; 🚇 4
The seductive stylings of owner-designers Thomas Schoos and Michael Berman – stone fireplaces, rippling fountains, flickering votives, elegant cabanas – entice passersby, but it's the exquisitely prepared dishes – Ironman steak salad, mahi mahi picatta – that close the deal. Pastry chef Meadow Lyn Ramsey's decadent desserts will ensure a second date.

### 🍴 SWEET LADY JANE Bakery $-$$
☎ 323-653-7145; www.sweetladyjane.com; 8360 Melrose Ave; ⏰ 8:30am-11:30pm Mon-Sat, 9:30am-4pm Sun; 🚇 MTA 10, 11; 🚻
There's a cake for every craving – orange chiffon, seven-layer chocolate, triple berry shortcake – inside the ivy-colored walls of Sweet Lady Jane, one of LA's most popular bakeries. To make the

choice even tougher, peek into the cake-making workshop to see what's frosting up next. Fresh sandwiches too.

## 🍸 DRINK

### 🍸 ABBEY Bar
☎ 310-289-8410; www.abbeyfoodandbar.com; 692 N Robertson Blvd; ⏰ 8am-2am; 🚇 MTA 220
Under the watchful eyes of gargoyles, this sprawling gothic monastery draws a sexually diverse West Hollywood crowd from sunrise to way past sunset. Since its opening 15 years ago as a tiny local coffee shop, the Abbey has expanded five times to its present incarnation as restaurant, bar and nightclub, complete with patios, cabanas and lounges. Plans for a Vegas Abbey are in the works. Wander next door for the buff boys and sleek designs of stylish Here (696 N Robertson Blvd), easy to miss in the shadows of the ongoing Abbey annexation.

### 🍸 ELIXIR TONICS & TEAS Tea
☎ 310-657-9300; www.elixirtonics.com; 8612 Melrose Ave; ⏰ 9am-10:30pm Mon-Thu, 9am-midnight Fri & Sat, 10am-10pm Sun; 🚇 MTA 10, 11
Tea is the new coffee at this teacup-sized retreat. Browse herbal tonics, candles and Buddhas, then order a freshly made tonic – try the Depth Recharger – at the tea bar.

NEIGHBORHOODS

WEST HOLLYWOOD

## HIPPER THAN THOU

So you want to go to the hottest clubs – Hyde Lounge, Les Doux? There's a trifecta of velvet-rope considerations. One, hotness is temporary. Two, bouncers can be aggressively unfriendly. Three, you may be standing on the sidewalk all night, and the celebutantes usually slip in the back. Still interested? If it's a trendy hotel bar, spending the night at the hotel or eating at the hotel's restaurant may help. No guarantees. For other scenester clubs, bring a blonde or be one, dress sharp, arrive early, and play it cool. Then go somewhere else after half an hour. As for Hyde Lounge, it's two doors down from **Greenblatt's Deli** ( ☎ 323-656-0606; 8017 Sunset Blvd) on the Strip – go order a pastrami on rye. It might be more enjoyable than the Hyde.

A secluded courtyard awaits those needing a longer zen moment.

### ▼ FORMOSA CAFÉ Bar
☎ 323-850-9050; www.formosacafe
.com; 7156 Santa Monica Blvd; ⏱ 4pm-2am Mon-Fri, 6pm-2am Sat & Sun;
🚌 MTA 10, 11

The lights are dim, the booths are comfy and the bar is low-key, perfect for Hollywood hipsters wanting to soak up the suds and the history – rumor has it Bogie drank here too. An approach-able Quentin Tarantino has been known to haunt the premises. Across the street, junior agents, baby execs and savvy assistants suck down cocktails in the shadows of dimly lit **Jones** ( ☎ 323-850-1727; 7201 Santa Monica Blvd), no longer the hippest kid around but still popular with Hollywood's young and harried. There's two degrees of separation between everyone here.

### ▼ SKYBAR Bar
☎ 323-848-6025; www.mondrianhotel
.com; 8440 W Sunset Blvd; ⏱ 11am-2am; 🚌 MTA 2

Like a fading diva still demanding her close-up, Skybar keeps the lines long on the Sunset sidewalk outside the Mondrian Hotel. But the wait's worth it – if just for the preening scene on the patio and gorgeous views of the twinkling city below. Gobs of impudent faux hawks and barely there dresses if you're looking.

### ▼ URTH CAFFÉ Coffeeshop
☎ 310-659-0628; www.urthcaffe.com;
⏱ 8565 Melrose Ave; 🚌 MTA 10, 11

The stylish and smart swoon over organic teas, coffees and pastries that are just possibly more posh than they are. Look sharp, the people-watching is intense and the vibe not always relaxing. Also in **Santa Monica** (Map pp96–7, D5; ☎ 310-314-7040; 2327 Main St).

# ⭐ PLAY

## ⭐ HOUSE OF BLUES
☎ 323-848-5100; www.hob.com; 8430 Sunset Blvd; 🚌 MTA 2

Despite a Disneyfied 'Mississippi blues shack' exterior, this center-of-the-strip music hall books quality, sometimes quirky, small-venue bands from all over the US and abroad.

## ⭐ RAGE
☎ 310-652-7055; www.ragewest hollywood.com; 8911 Santa Monica Blvd; 🚌 MTA 4

Buff bods and the boys who love them groove to the music on DJ-driven dance floors at this high-energy club, while scenesters check each other out on the sizzling sidewalk patio. Check the website for theme nights and drink specials.

## ⭐ TROUBADOUR
☎ 310-276-6168; www.troubadour.com; 9081 Santa Monica Blvd; 🚌 MTA 4

A mix of rock legends, cult faves and MySpace up-and-comers keep the rafters rising at this legendary rock hall – open since 1957 – where a beer-drinking crowd serious about its music keeps attitude to a minimum. Bob Dylan, Joni Mitchell, James Taylor and Guns N' Roses played early gigs here.

House of Blues puts up bands from far and wide

# >MID-CITY

Once considered a low-key launch pad for adventure elsewhere, Mid-City has become one of LA's newest high-profile destinations. The recently opened Park La Brea apartment complex has infused the neighborhood with an upwardly mobile crowd ready to spend some cash. And that they're doing, across the street at The Grove, an Italian-style outdoor mall perpetually packed with shoppers and people-watchers since opening in 2002. The inimitable Farmers Market, with its produce and food stalls, chugs along next door, basking in newfound glory-by-association – though it essentially hasn't changed since 1934.

Foodies flock for the latest ventures – AOC, Pizzeria Mozza, M Café de Chaya – from some of LA's most inventive chefs. Boutiques pop up monthly along 3rd St and antique-sellers on La Brea Ave still reel in bargain-hunters. On Wilshire's Museum Row, LACMA relishes a much-needed expansion while tar buffs and car buffs wander the La Brea Tar Pits and Petersen Automotive Museum.

## MID-CITY

### ⊙ SEE
La Brea Tar Pits..............1  D5
Los Angeles County Museum
of Art ..............................2  D5
Page Museum ..............(see 1)
Petersen Automotive
Museum ........................3  C5

### 🏠 SHOP
American Rag..................4  E4
Beverly Center................5  A4
Cook's Library............(see 10)
Larchmont Ave ..............6  H4
Munky King ....................7  E2

Polka Dots &
Moonbeams ..............(see 10)
Remix Vintage Shoes .....8  D3
The Grove ......................9  D4
Travelers Bookcase.......10  B4
Wasteland ....................11  D2

### 🍴 EAT
AOC ..............................12  C4
Buddha's Belly...............13  D3
Campanile .....................14  E5
Doughboys ...................15  C4
Farmers Market.............16  C4
M Café de Chaya ..........17  E2
Pink's ............................18  E2

Pizzeria Mozza .............19  F2
Tere's Mexican Grill ......20  G2
Toast Bakery Café.........21  B4
Village Idiot..................22  E2

### 🍸 DRINK
El Coyote Mexican
Café ..............................23  E3
Tom Bergin's Tavern.....24  C6

### ⭐ PLAY
Groundlings ................25  E2

Please see over for map

Browsing the bookstore at LACMA's Japanese Pavilion

# SEE

## LA BREA TAR PITS & PAGE MUSEUM

☎ 323-934-7243; www.tarpits.org; 5801 Wilshire Blvd; museum adult/senior, student & 13-17yr/5-12yr/under 5yr $7/4.50/2/free, tar pits only free; 9:30am-5pm Mon-Fri, 10am-5pm Sat & Sun; MTA 20, 21; P ♿ 👶

The low-grade oil bubbling at the corner of Wilshire and Curson was formed over millions of years as the remains of ancient sea life merged with marine sediments to form fossil fuels. As oceans receded and land emerged, this 'tar' would seep to the surface, ensnaring animals unfortunate enough to get caught in its sticky mire. Scientists collect, clean and catalog these ancient remains –

watch them in the Fishbowl Laboratory – and display some of the most amazing within the museum. Staff are disturbingly vague about recent, perhaps apocryphal, stories of lost mid-city pooches. Parking costs $6. See also p21.

## LOS ANGELES COUNTY MUSEUM OF ART

LACMA; ☎ 323-857-6000; www.lacma .org; 5905 Wilshire Blvd; adult/senior & student/under 17yr $9/5/free, free after 5pm & all day 2nd Tue of month; noon-8pm Mon, Tue & Thu, noon-9pm Fri, 11am-8pm Sat & Sun; MTA 20, 21; P ♿

Exploring LACMA's almost overwhelming permanent collections, it occasionally seems that sponsors receive more prominent labeling than the exhibits. Just embrace

the largesse and focus on the astounding scope of the museum's holdings, scattered across six buildings. Diego Rivera's *Flower Day*, Rembrandt's *Portrait of Maerten Looten*, Southeast Asian and Islamic art (the last, perhaps not surprisingly, in the Getty Oil Gallery) and the contemporary collection are highlights, as are the impressionist and postimpressionist paintings and sculptures. LACMA is undergoing a major, much-needed renovation and expansion. Expect by late 2007 a new contemporary art building, a 60ft by 60ft performance stage, and more open space and piazzas. You'll have the place to yourself Friday afternoons. Parking costs $6.

**PETERSEN AUTOMOTIVE MUSEUM**
☎ 323-930-2277; www.petersen .org; 6060 Wilshire Blvd; adult/senior & student/5-12yr $10/5/3; ☼ 10am-6pm Tue-Sun; 🚍 MTA 20, 21
With the main entrance opening onto the parking garage, cars get their due at this four-story ode to the auto. Wander past a 1903 Cadillac, a 1923 UPS truck and a 2006 Bugatti – from zero to 60 in 2.5 seconds – as well as accessible displays fascinating for know-it-alls and newbies alike. Picture-taking welcome.

# 🛍 SHOP

In addition to the open-air mall madness of The Grove, the surrounding Mid-City blocks are dotted with boutiques and specialty stores. Check out 3rd St just east of La Cienega for one-of-a-kind boutiques, bookstores and cafés. For antiques as well as boutiques, try La Brea Ave south of Melrose Ave, and for a cute, small-town vibe, wander Larchmont Ave near Hancock Park, where you might just see a favorite TV star noshing with family on a sidewalk patio.

**AMERICAN RAG**
*Boutique/Vintage Clothing*
☎ 323-935-3154; 150 S La Brea Ave; ☼ 10am-9pm Mon-Sat, noon-7pm Sun; 🚍 212
Tiny tees, tight jeans and top-tier brands make this chic store a fave with the MySpace crowd. The

---

**GIVE YOUR CAR TO A COMPLETE STRANGER**
Parking is at a premium in LA, and valets are here to alleviate the parking stress. Don't waste too much time driving around the block in a strange city, just accept the reality. Hand over the keys, keep the ticket, and collect your car a few hours later. Just remember to keep spare cash handy for the end of the night. Costs can range from $3.50 to upwards of $10, plus tip.

latest designer duds are on the left while vintage, slightly cheaper 'rags' are found on the right. Saucy shoes preen in the middle.

### ☐ BEVERLY CENTER *Mall*

☎ 310-854-0071; www.beverlycenter .com; 8500 Beverly Blvd; ⏰ 10am-9pm Mon-Fri, 10am-8pm Sat, 11am-6pm Sun; 🚍 MTA 14; Ⓟ

Despite the Soviet-style exterior, this is LA's glamour mall, easily accessed by Hollywood Hills celebs in need of one-stop shopping. Show your hotel key at guest services for discounts, then lose yourself in over 160 boutique shops, department stores and restaurants. Parking costs $1 for the first three hours.

### ☐ THE GROVE *Outdoor Mall*

☎ 888-315-8883; www.thegrovela.com; 189 The Grove Dr; ⏰ 10am-9pm Mon-Thu, 10am-10pm Fri & Sat, 11am-8pm Sun; 🚍 MTA 16, 217; Ⓟ

This outdoor mall is one of LA's most popular shopping destinations. Its recipe for success? Fill a faux Italian palazzo with 40 name-brand stores and restaurants, toss in a fountain, the Pacific Theatres and a sprinkling of celebrities, then top it off with a trolley rolling back and forth down the middle. PT Barnum would be proud. Check out the roof of the parking garage for stellar city views. Highlights include little-girl fave American Girl Place and grown-up-gal boutique

Plenty of riches at American Rag

### Jim Marshall
*Charlie Sheen's stand-in on* Two and a Half Men, *actor and movie-house connoisseur*

**What exactly does Charlie Sheen's stand-in do?** The director sets shots with us and the cameraman…Once set, we do it with dialogue at full speed. **What's best about the job?** It's a crash course in writing, directing and acting. From ground zero I get to watch all the processes unfold. **Any tips for sitting in the studio audience?** Dress in layers; sound stages are air-conditioned and really cold. **Where's the best place to grab dinner after a hard day at the studio?** Tere's Mexican Grill (p80) on Melrose. It's good authentic Mexican food and you'll see actors there. **Who's got the best burger?** The Bowery (p47) on Sunset. Get it with the works. When I bit into it, I thought, this is not just the best burger, but it's the best burger I've had in five years. **What's the best thing about living in LA?** The breadth of screenings available at LACMA (p71), the Egyptian (p50), and the Motion Picture Academy. On good prints, too.

Theodore. Parking free for the first hour; $3 for two to three hours.

### ☐ POLKA DOTS & MOONBEAMS *Clothing*
☎ 323-655-3880; www.polkadots andmoonbeams.com; 8381 W 3rd St; ☽ 11am-7pm Mon-Sat, to 5pm Sun; ☐ MTA 16

Stylistas sing the praises of this sassy number where orange Juicy jackets mingle with lime Free the People tees. From up-and-coming designers to fashionable old faves, there's something – bright sun-dresses, short shorts and spunky shoes – for every occasion. Check out the still-bursting-with-style **vintage shop** ( ☎ 323-651-1746; 8367 W 3rd St) a few doors down.

### ☐ REMIX VINTAGE SHOES
*Shoes*
☎ 323-936-6210; 7605 Beverly Blvd; ☽ noon-7pm Mon-Sat, to 6pm Sun; ☐ MTA 14

Feet feeling retro? Check out the never-worn vintage and reproduction footwear from the 1940s to '60s sold here. From baby-doll pumps or two-tone wingtips, your feet will be trippin' the light fantastic.

### ☐ TRAVELERS BOOKCASE
*Books*
☎ 323-655-0575; www.travelbooks .com; 8375 W 3rd St; ☽ 10am-6pm Mon-Sat, 11am-5pm Sun; ☐ MTA 16; Ⓟ

Sate your travel palate at tiny Travelers Bookcase, where day-trippers and vagabonds alike find it hard to leave empty-handed. Guidebooks, adventure lit and chick-trip tomes camp out in front while maps, sanitizers and yoga mats loiter in back. At **Cook's Library** ( ☎ 323-655-3141; www.cooks library.com; 8373 W 3rd St) next door, cuisine queens and toast-burners alike savor cookbooks, how-tos and dining guides.

### ☐ WASTELAND *Clothing*
☎ 323-653-3028; 7428 Melrose Ave; ☽ 11am-8pm Mon-Sat, to 7pm Sun; ☐ MTA 10, 11

Vintage kingpin Wasteland towers over the Melrose shopping scene from its perch at the corner of Vista St and Melrose Ave. Glamour gowns, velvet suits and last season's designs fill the endless racks.

# 🍴 EAT

## 🍽 AOC *Mediterranean Tapas* $$$
☎ 323-653-6359; www.aocwinebar
.com; 8022 W 3rd St; ⏱ 6-11pm Mon-Fri,
5:30-11pm Sat, 5:30-10pm Sun; 🚌 MTA
16; Ⓥ
Stylish AOC glows like the cozy
wine cellar of a very good, very
rich friend. With over 50 wines
by the glass, a three-page list of
savory tapas and a welcoming but
discreet vibe, AOC easily remains
a consistent favorite of couples,
friends and groups alike, not to
mention the typically fickle Hollywood hoi polloi. Reservations
recommended.

## 🍽 BUDDHA'S BELLY
*Pan-Asian*                          $-$$
☎ 323-931-8588; www.bbfood.com;
7475 Beverly Blvd; ⏱ noon-10pm Mon-
Thu, noon-11pm Fri & Sat, 3-10pm Sun;
🚌 MTA 14
This bright, bamboo-accented corner eatery serves accessible Asian
to an upscale but unpretentious
crowd. With an enticing array of
noodles, curries and broths, it can
be tough to make up your mind.
Come early or make reservations,
as this busy Buddha fills up quick.

## 🍽 CAMPANILE *Cal-French*   $$$
☎ 323-938-1447; www.campanile
restaurant.com; 624 S La Brea Ave;
⏱ 11:30am-2:30pm Mon-Fri, 6-10pm
Mon-Wed, 5:30-11pm Thu-Sat, 9:30am-
1:30pm Sat & Sun; 🚌 212; ♿ 🚶
Occupying a spot in the city's culinary pantheon for over 15 years,
chef-owner Mark Peel knows how
to turn market-fresh ingredients
into beautiful dishes. For more
casual dining, stop by for Thursday's popular Grilled Cheese Night
and sample one of 12 traditional
and not-so-traditional sandwiches
created with LA flair and Campanile
care. Reservations recommended.

## 🍽 DOUGHBOYS *Bakery Café*   $
☎ 323-651-4202; 8136 W 3rd St;
⏱ 7am-midnight; 🚌 16
If Oprah formed a Cupcake Club,
her Doughboy's favorite – the Red
Velvet – would surely be asked to
join. This cream-cheese-frosted
diet-buster joins similar naughty
items served up quick at this boho-
artist redoubt. The concrete floor
and wooden-tables don't detract
from the creatively prepared soups
and sandwiches. Portions are huge.

## 🍽 FARMERS MARKET
*Farmers Market*                     $
☎ 323-933-9211; www.farmersmarket
la.com; 6333 W 3rd St; ⏱ 9am-9pm
Mon-Fri, 9am-8pm Sat, 10am-7pm Sun;
🚌 MTA 16; Ⓟ ♿ Ⓥ 🚶
With 70 shops and stalls offering
an international array of foods,
the Farmers Market is a vibrant
crossroads of cultures and cuisines.

Pink's landmark hot-dog stand

Established in 1934, the market was immediately popular with the community and has remained so ever since. The mouthwatering tacos at **Loteria Grill** ( ☎ 323-930-2211) and the spicy gumbo yaya at the **Gumbo Pot** ( ☎ 323-933-0358) are worth a bite.

### ✗ M CAFÉ DE CHAYA
*Macrobiotic* $-$$

☎ 323-525-0588; www.mcafedechaya .com; 7119 Melrose Ave; ☼ 9am-10pm Mon-Sat, 9am-9pm Sun; 🚌 MTA 10, 11; P V

Place your order at the counter then grab a spot at one of the tightly packed two tops at this bright but narrow eatery where the people-watching can be intense. The menu is macrobiotic – natural whole foods eaten in

season – and primarily vegetarian except for tuna and shrimp. The grilled tuna burger and organic fries are especially keen. Celeb-spotting potential is off the charts.

### ✗ PINK'S *American Fast Food* $
☎ 323-931-4223; 709 N La Brea Ave; ☼ 9:30am-2am Sun-Thu, 9:30am-3am Fri & Sat; 🚌 MTA 212; ♿ ⚤

The Black Dahlia, David Hasselhoff, and the line at Pink's – these are LA's enduring mysteries. Lunch, dinner, late night, there's always a line at this family-owned, wood-and-concrete hot-dog stand that's been around since 1939. Half the fun may be the anticipation – biting a chili-and-cheese-slathered dog for the signature 'snap' is definitely worth, uh, an hour-long wait?

## WHAT TO DO IF YOU SEE A STAR

The odds of seeing a star in the 30-mile zone surrounding Hollywood are actually pretty good. So what should you do if you happen upon Brad, Halle or Reese? Follow these pointers to maximize your celeb-spotting experience:

1. Respect their personal space. Take stock of your surroundings and remember you're looking at a person, not a product. George Clooney is a living, breathing human being. Yes, he sells movies but he's not a can of soda (though he may be a bag of chips). Piercing shrieks and convulsive hyperventilating can be off-putting.

2. Don't mimic their most famous catchphrase. Jake Gyllenhaal doesn't want to hear 'I wish I knew how to quit you!' yelled across the ArcLight lobby in a faux cowboy accent. Although imitation is the sincerest form of flattery, it's not always polite. And he's probably heard it before.

3. Don't comment on their height or lack thereof. Most stars are short. Some are very short. Understanding this before entering Hollywood will work in your favor. Blurting, 'Wow, you're a lot shorter in real life!' at Orlando Bloom in Runyon Canyon will endear you to no one.

4. Compliment their work. Everyone loves a compliment, and stars are no different.

### 🍴 PIZZERIA MOZZA
*Pizza*     $$-$$$
☎ 323-297-0101; www.mozza-la.com; 641 N Highland Ave; 🕑 noon-midnight; 🚌 MTA 10, 11; Ⓥ

'At the table, one never gets old,' is the motto on the menu here. How true. But old age comes when you're trying to score a reservation at this booked-for-weeks posh pizzeria from Nancy Silverton and Mario Batali. The fennel sausage, prosciutto and salami are indicative of the high-fat, high-taste toppings that gourmands and groupies demand. No reservation? Come in early for a seat at the bar. Sister-venture Osteria Mozza will be opening soon.

### 🍴 TERE'S MEXICAN GRILL
*Mexican*     $
☎ 323-468-9345; 5870 W Melrose Ave; 🕑 9am-9pm Mon-Sat; 🚌 MTA 10, 11; 🚼

Tucked in an easy-to-miss mini-mall near Paramount Studios, Tere's may be no-frills, but its authentic Mexican grub draws a heavy stream of 'to-go' traffic from hungry hipsters and harried homemakers alike. Eclectic South of the Border decor, drink crates and tightly packed two-tops crowd the small space but happy noshers don't seem to notice these distractions.

### 🍴 TOAST BAKERY CAFÉ
*American*     $-$$
☎ 323-655-5018; 8221 W 3rd St; 🕑 7:30am-10pm; 🚌 MTA 16; Ⓥ 🚼

From sitcom stars to dolly grips, the Hollywood crowd loves its Toast. Not to mention its tasty egg scrambles, luscious pancakes and frothy lattes. This popular eatery recently added dinner hours, so avoid the crush on weekend mornings and stop by for an evening bite.

### VILLAGE IDIOT
*American Gastropub* $$
☎ 323-655-3331; 7383 Melrose Ave; 🕑 11:30am-11pm daily, late-night menu 11pm-midnight Sun-Thu & 11pm-1am Fri & Sat; 🚌 MTA 10, 11
Delish comfort food, upbeat staff and a welcoming vibe draw the smart crowd to the soaring wood-and-brick walls of the newest eatery on Melrose. Although the busy wait staff can be stretched a bit thin, idiots and gastronomes alike don't mind seem to mind after biting into juicy burgers and fluffy fish and chips, the latter some of the best in town.

## 🍸 DRINK

### EL COYOTE MEXICAN CAFÉ
*Mexican Bar*
☎ 323-939-2255; www.elcoyotecafe .com; 7312 Beverly Blvd; 🕑 11am-10pm Sun-Mon, to 11pm Fri & Sat; 🚌 MTA 14
With 24 tequilas and a variety of margaritas prominently displayed on the menu, there's no doubt what's pulling 'em in at this

festive, red-boothed institution where Sharon Tate is rumored to have eaten her last meal. Pay a buck more for the tastier home-made 'scratch' margarita, but word to the wise: drinks here are fall-on-your-face strong. Witnesses can attest.

### 🍸 TOM BERGIN'S TAVERN
*Irish Pub*
☎ 323-936-7151; www.tombergins .com; 840 S Fairfax Ave; 🕑 11:30am-2am; 🚌 MTA 217
Every neighborhood needs a Tom Bergin's. Fish and chips, chatty barflies, and plenty of Guinness and Irish coffee. Rumor has it that the wooden, U-shaped bar was the inspiration for the one seen on *Cheers*. And of course the St Paddy's Day celebration isn't to be missed.

## ⭐ PLAY

### ⭐ GROUNDLINGS *Comedy*
☎ 323-934-4747; www.groundlings .com; 7307 Melrose Ave; admission $10-20; 🕑 box office 10am-6pm Mon-Tue, 10am-8pm Wed & Thu, 10am-10pm Fri & Sat, noon-7:30pm Sun; 🚌 MTA 10, 11
From sketch to improv, the much-kudoed Groundlings comedy troupe conjures up the funny every night. Surprise guests who've gone on to *Saturday Night Live* and *Mad TV* often drop by Thursday nights.

# >BEVERLY HILLS & WESTSIDE

Beverly Hills cuts through Los Angeles like the grandest of royal cruise ships. Glittering streets, chic boutiques and posh restaurants – all sparkle on her haughty decks with the security and charm befitting the securely monied. The Getty Center and Hammer Museum provide the artistic backdrop while the Museum of Television & Radio offers a buffet of multimedia distractions. The upscale living quarters are also perfectly appointed, but typically off-limits to the cabin class.

But the queen has felt a ripple; a party barge from a neighborhood to the south, known as Culver City, has disturbed the upper-class waters, rollicking on the bouncy wake. Carrying young artists, funky galleries, entrepreneurs, gritty bars and a whiff of impudent energy, this up-and-comer is hogging the spotlight. Some sniff it's not even really part of the Westside. But it is the new, new place, and most say it's right on time.

## BEVERLY HILLS & WESTSIDE

# SEE

## GETTY CENTER

☎ 310-440-7300; www.getty.edu; 1200 Getty Center Dr, off I-405; admission free; ⏱ 10am-6pm Tue-Thu & Sun, to 9pm Fri & Sat; 🚌 761; 🅿

For optimal Getty pleasure, plan to spend at least half a day wandering the pavilions, gardens and viewpoints that fill this hillside haven. Be sure to include time for the drive to the museum, the tram ride and a bit of orientation once you reach the arrival plaza and entrance hall. Pavilions 1 through 4 hold the permanent collections while displays on the 2nd floor of the Exhibitions Pavilion change periodically. For Roman and Greek

## CULVER CITY GALLERIES

Gallery-hopping in Culver City is the current must-do, with 30 galleries jostling for space along Washington Blvd and La Cienega Blvd south of the I-10 (Santa Monica Fwy). The renaissance began in 2003 when **Blum & Poe** (2754 S La Cienega Blvd), with its roster of well-known artists, moved from the comfy confines of Santa Monica to the once-industrial blocks of La Cienega. **Lightbox** (2656 S La Cienega Blvd), **LAXART** (2640 S LaCienega Blvd) and other artist-friendly enterprises followed. Bars and restaurants are still opening, the first Art Walk drew 1500 people, and the Exposition light-rail line is set to open in 2010. Before you know it, the artists will be gone, looking for the next new thing.

Richard Meier–designed Getty Center

antiquities, visit the **Getty Villa** ( ☎ 310-440-7300; www.getty.edu; 17985 Pacific Coast Hwy; admission free, reservations required; ⏰ 10am-5pm Thu-Mon; Ⓟ ). Parking for both places costs $8.

## 💿 GREYSTONE MANSION & PARK

☎ 310-550-4654; 905 Loma Vista Dr; admission free; ⏰ 10am-5pm Oct-Mar, 10am-6pm Apr-Sep; 🚌 MTA 2, 302, 305; Ⓟ ♿

Spooky Greystone Mansion, with its stone walls and balustrades, seems more suited for foggy Scottish bluffs than shiny Beverly Hills – even the cleaning crews hurry to clear out by sunset. Why? The gothic-style mansion was the site of the still-mysterious 1929 murder of oil heir Ned Doheny and may be recognizable from *Ghostbusters II* and *The Witches of Eastwick*. The home is closed but the gardens and grounds are open. Citywide views from the front patio are stellar.

Spooky statue at the Greystone Mansion

## 💿 HAMMER MUSEUM

☎ 310-443-7000; www.hammer.ucla .edu; 10899 Wilshire Blvd; adult/senior/ student & under 17yr $5/3/free, free on Thu; ⏰ 11am-7pm Tue, Wed, Fri & Sat, to 9pm Thu, to 5pm Sun; 🚌 20, 21, 720

## THE MUSEUM OF JURASSIC TECHNOLOGY

From the moment you ring the outside bell, you know something's up. Inside the **Museum of Jurassic Technology** ( ☎ 310-836-6131; www.mjt.org; 9341 Venice Blvd, Culver City), you won't find a pamphlet, just a short introductory film that's…well, maybe just wing it and watch your mind fracture as you wander this whacked-out warren masterminded by MacArthur Fellow David Wilson. A gallery honoring Russian space dogs? The Pope in the eye of a needle? The myth of mice on toast? You'll either giggle or run for the door, but you won't read a museum plaque with any certainty again. See for yourself, though: in keeping with the museum's spirit, this review may not be accurate.

Fancy a fine-art immersion – but need it fast? Step off the busy streets of Westwood and indulge in the collections of entrepreneur Armand Hammer. Nineteenth-century French masters – Gaugin, Monet, Manet, Pissaro and Van Gogh – and a noteworthy collection of Honore Daumier caricatures of French society are highlights.

### MUSEUM OF TELEVISION & RADIO

☎ 310-786-1000; www.mtr.org; 465 N Beverly Dr; admission free; ✆ noon-5pm Wed-Sun; 🚌 MTA 20, 21, 720; 🅿

This sweeping glass-and-stone landmark by Getty designer Richard Meier holds cultural treasures as captivating as the building itself. Scan the collections list, pick your TV or radio fave, then grab a seat at a console and enjoy. Media addicts beware: with more than 100,000 donated programs, from early Burns & Allen to the moon walk to Secretariat's triple crown win, you could be here a while. Parking is validated for two hours.

### WESTWOOD MEMORIAL PARK

☎ 310-474-1579; 1218 Glendon Ave; admission free; ✆ 8am-dusk; 🚌 20, 21, 720

Half the challenge is finding this postage stamp–sized cemetery. Tucked behind a commercial building, celebrity-filled Westwood Memorial seems the current Hyde Lounge of the post-life set. Truman Capote, Dean Martin and Marilyn Monroe – see the lipstick prints – crowd sanctuaries near the entrance while headstones for rabble rousers like Rodney 'There goes the neighborhood' Dangerfield keep 'em chuckling in back.

# SHOP

Glamour, Glitz, and Elegance frolic among immaculate streets and sparkling windows on Rodeo Dr, where a roll-call of Italian finery and fashion commands two fabulous blocks, all culminating in a corner

Celebrity-filled Westwood Memorial Park

NEIGHBORHOODS

BEVERLY HILLS & WESTSIDE

## EARTHQUAKES OF FASHION

The new **Prada** (343 N Rodeo Dr) 'epicenter' on Rodeo is as much about ogling as shopping. The 24,000ft showroom, designed by Dutch architect Rem Koolhouse, yawns directly onto the sidewalk like the world's haughtiest garage. Inside, faceless fembots, all fabulously frocked, pretend they have something better to do.

of couture known simply as Two Rodeo. From surrounding streets, upscale chains and department stores flirt like shameless courtiers, ready to please your every whim – for just the right price.

### BARNEYS NEW YORK
*Department Store*
☎ 310-276-4400; 9570 Wilshire Blvd; ☼ 10am-7pm Mon-Wed, Fri & Sat, to 8pm Thu, noon- 6pm Sun; 🚌 MTA 20, 21, 720
A grand central staircase woos shoppers through four floors of svelte and stylish designer duds for every possible occasion. The best part? Lunch at rooftop deli-with-a-view, Barney Greengrass.

### CENTURY CITY *Outdoor Mall*
☎ 310-277-3898; www.westfield.com/centurycity; 10250 Santa Monica Blvd; ☼ 10am-9pm Mon-Sat, 11am-6pm Sun; 🚌 MTA 28, BBB5; 🅿 ♿

A divine alfresco shopping mall, and it's only a mile from Rodeo Dr. Godiva, Kenneth Cole and Abercrombie & Fitch are among more than 200 mostly high-end stores anchored by Bloomingdales and Macy's. New shops, restaurants and a dining terrace were added in 2005 as part of a long-term renovation. Parking free for three hours.

### CHEESE STORE OF BEVERLY HILLS *Cheese*
☎ 310-278-2855; www.cheesestorebh.com; 419 N Beverly Dr, Beverly Hills; ☼ 10am-6pm Mon-Sat; 🚌 MTA 20, 21, 720
If someone moved your cheese, you're likely to find it – or something better – at this charming, well-stocked *fromagerie*. French, Italian, aged, new, hard or soft – all jockey for attention from the counter while wine, olives and oils call out from towering shelves.

### HARRY WINSTON *Jewelry*
☎ 310-271-8554; 310 N Rodeo Dr; ☼ 10am-6pm Mon-Fri, 11am-5pm Sat, noon-5pm Sun; 🚌 MTA 20, 21, 720
The priciest store on Rodeo may be the happiest to see you. After a recent move to brighter, more accessible digs, the famed diamond purveyor replaced its formal counters with small islands to improve pedestrian flow. Silk velvet and silver leaf adorn the

soaring walls, complementing the still-stunning array of sparkling baubles.

### LULULEMON *Athletic Wear*
☎ 310-858-8339; www.lululemon.com; 334 N Beverly Dr; 🕲 10am-7pm Mon-Fri, to 8pm Sat, 11am-6pm Sun; 🚌 MTA 20, 21, 720

Yoga lovers yen for Lululemon's zen – where fashionable yogawear and knowledgeable staff quicken your search for perfect peace, not to mention the most flattering pair of workout pants. Wary about the yoga thing? This upbeat, colorful store offers free one-day classes on Sundays. Newbies encouraged.

# 🍴 EAT

### 🍴 CRUSTACEAN
*Eurasian* $$$-$$$$
☎ 310-205-8990; www.anfamily .com; 9646 Little Santa Monica Blvd; 🕲 11:30am-2:30pm Mon-Fri, 5:30-10:30pm Mon-Thu, 5:30-11:30pm Fri & Sat, 4-9pm Sun; 🚌 MTA 16

Push through the posh French Colonial doors and follow the glass-covered koi pond to the elegant but accessible main dining room. Favorites on the seafood-centric menu include drunken crab, royal tiger prawns and garlic noodles or garlic mashed potatoes. Reservations recommended.

Plentiful supply at the Cheese Store of Beverly Hills

**Linda Welton with map co-seller Shae Lyons**
*Owner of Star Maps at corner of Sunset Blvd & Baroda Dr*

**How long has your family been selling maps?** Since 1936… My mom was out here 45 years. **What's the coolest part of your job?** I like it because it's the only job I can think of where everyone comes up in an excited, great mood. **Have any stars said hello?** Dr Phil stops and talks to us. **Whose home is most requested?** They ask for Jessica Simpson. **Whose houses are good for viewing?** Ten minutes away are Tobey Maguire, Keanu Reeves, Leo DiCaprio and Justin Timberlake – all homes are visible… Sidney Poitier's is beautiful. On the corner and gorgeous. **Who's being added to the next map?** We got Brad Pitt, Angelina Jolie in Malibu…the Ashton Kutcher and Demi Moore home, Ashlee Simpson and the new Sharon Stone home.

## GRILL ON THE ALLEY
*American*                              $$$-$$$$

☎ 310-276-0615; www.thegrill.com;
9650 Dayton Way; ⏰ 11:30am-11pm
Mon-Thu, 11:30am-midnight Fri & Sat,
5-9pm Sun; 🚌 720

When they say 'Let's do lunch,'
this is where they do it. Wood-
paneled walls, framed portraits,
see-and-be-seen booths and
white-jacketed waitstaff lend a
Golden Age flair to the A-lister
power scene. Succulent Kobe beef
burgers, towering cobb salads and
the 'orgasmic' John Dory are faves.
Reservations recommended.

## MULBERRY STREET
PIZZERIA *Pizza*                              $

☎ 310-247-8100; www.mulberrypizza
.com; 240 S Beverly Dr; ⏰ 11am-11pm

Sun-Thu, 11am-midnight Fri & Sat;
🚌 MTA 20, 21, 720; ♿

Regularly voted one of LA's best
pizza joints, this red-checkered,
low-attitude respite is the spot
for New York–style slices – thin,
greasy and served up quick.

## NATE & AL'S *Deli*                              $-$$

☎ 310-274-0101; www.natenal.com;
414 N Beverly Dr; ⏰ 7am-9pm Mon-Sun;
🚌 20, 21, 720; ♿

At this old-school, 'You want the
pastrami?' deli, you'll feel like a local
the moment you slide into a worn,
rust-colored booth. Dapper seniors,
chatty sisters, loud-mouthed stunt-
men, and even Larry King – everybody's stopped by at some point.
Loxes, blintzes, omelets, briskets
and knishes, served up since 1945.

Hearty fare at Nate & Al's

NEIGHBORHOODS

BEVERLY HILLS & WESTSIDE

Splurge at Spago

### 🍴 SPAGO Cal-Italian $$$$

☎ 310-385-0880; www.wolfgangpuck
.com; 176 N Canon Dr; ⏱ 11:30am-
2:15pm Mon-Fri, noon-2:30pm Sat,
5:30-10:30pm Sun-Thu, 5:30-11pm Fri &
Sat; Ⓜ 20, 21, 720; ♿ Ⓥ

The primped and the powdered
preen inside the glass-encrusted
patio like poodles at Westminster.
There's nary a hair out of place as
they nibble on smoked salmon
pizza, pan-roasted milk-fed
veal rib chops, Cantonese-style
roasted duck and other long-
winded kibbles and bits. Is an LA
travel guide definitive without a
nod to Wolfgang Puck's paean to
extravagant dining? Not today.
But soon.

### 🍴 SPRINKLES CUPCAKES
*Bakery* $

☎ 310-274-8765; www.sprinkles
cupcakes.com; 9635 Little Santa Monica
Blvd; ⏱ 9am-7pm Mon-Sat, 10am-6pm
Sun; 🚌 20, 21, 720; ♿

Pay $3.25 for a cupcake? And you
have to wait in that line out the
door? Are you kidding – hey, that
looks pretty good. Red Velvet?
With cream cheese frosting? And
that one? Peanut butter chocolate?
Eighteen more varieties inside?
Uhh, can you move over a little?

### 🍴 TENDER GREENS
*Health Food* $

☎ 310-842-8300; www.tendergreens
food.com; 9523 Culver Blvd, Culver City;

⏱ 11:30am-9pm Sun-Thu, 11:30am-10pm Fri & Sat; 🚇 MTA 220; 🚫 Ⓥ ♿ At Culver City's latest hotspot, lines regularly spill out the door. Exclusive nightclub? Nope, it's Tender Greens, home of the freshest salads in the city. Order at the bright counter – try ahi tuna niçoise or grilled flatiron steak – and they'll toss it up as you move down the line. There's a whiff of salad nazi in the prep – 'We don't recommend substitutions' – but trust them, they're that good.

# 🍸 DRINK

### Ⓨ MANDRAKE *Bar*
☎ 310-837-3297; www.mandrakebar .com; 2692 S La Cienega Blvd, Culver City; ⏱ 2pm-midnight Sun-Thu, to 1am Fri & Sat

Remember those parties in high school, chillin' in somebody's parent's garage – concrete floor, a little cold, a work-in-progress kinda place – where you were ready to drop your cup and run at the first sign of trouble? Mandrake's got that garage-cool feel plus a couple of art chicks. Opened by an art-minded trio in the heart of Culver

City's gallery district, this little bar's got a big buzz. And it's fun.

### Ⓨ NIC'S BEVERLY HILLS *Bar*
☎ 310-550-5707; www.nicsbeverlyhills .com; 453 N Canon Dr; ⏱ 5pm-close; 🚌 20, 21, 720

Martinis for every palate lure the cocktail crowd to upscale but fun-loving Nic's, where the libations range from the colorful and sassy to the no-frills and classy. Reserve the chilled VodBox for flights of international vodka. Lounge bands Friday and Saturday night.

### Ⓨ POLO LOUNGE AT THE BEVERLY HILLS HOTEL *Bar*
☎ 1-800-283-8885; www.thebeverly hillshotel.com; 9641 Sunset Blvd; ⏱ 7am-1:30am; 🚌 2, 320, 305; Ⓟ With its mix of tennis whites, business suits and chi-chi dresses, this swanky, wood-paneled watering hole has the feel of a Hollywood country club. From smiling Isaac Mizrahi to still-tan George Hamilton to scruffy David Arquette, you never know who you'll see murmuring in the perpetually reserved, dark booths. This is the place to sip a martini in Old Hollywood style.

# >SANTA MONICA

Sunny Santa Monica is the quintessential West Coast beach town – wide glistening beaches, stylish shopping enclaves, saladcentric eateries and an affluent population that hangs on to its socially conscious, laid-back roots. Just don't smoke on the beach.

Montana Ave is the chicest of the shopping districts, lined for blocks with boutiques specializing in upscale designs for women, babies and puppies. Main St offers a similar small-town charm, though the fashions and attitudes trend toward beachy casual, while Third St Promenade, with its loitering teens, chain stores and street performers, has a slightly edgier vibe.

The beaches serve up the same mix of affluent and anything goes. Top-notch hotels and restaurants line the oceanfront where the rich and remote can watch sunsets from behind the safety of glass walls. Those preferring the arena to the stands head to the beach for bike riding, bodyboarding and volleyball, or to the Santa Monica Pier for the solar-powered Ferris wheel (but preferably not after dark, when the scene gets a bit sketchier).

## SANTA MONICA

### ◉ SEE
| | | |
|---|---|---|
| Bergamot Station | 1 | F2 |
| Camera Obscura | 2 | B4 |
| Pacific Park | 3 | B4 |
| Palisades Park | 4 | B3 |
| Perry's Café | 5 | A3 |
| Perry's Café | 6 | B3 |
| Perry's Café | 7 | C5 |
| Perry's Café | 8 | D5 |
| Santa Monica Pier | 9 | B4 |
| Santa Monica Pier Aquarium | 10 | B4 |
| Santa Monica State Beach | 11 | C5 |
| Santa Monica State Beach | 12 | B4 |

### 🛍 SHOP
| | | |
|---|---|---|
| Babystyle | 13 | C2 |
| Black + Blue | 14 | D5 |
| Blonde LA | 15 | D5 |
| Hear Music | 16 | C4 |
| Horizons West | 17 | C5 |
| Puzzle Zoo | 18 | C4 |
| Undefeated | 19 | D5 |
| Whimsy Alley | 20 | D1 |

### 🍴 EAT
| | | |
|---|---|---|
| Café Montana | 21 | C1 |
| Counter | 22 | G3 |
| El Cholo | 23 | C2 |
| Hump | 24 | H3 |
| Library Alehouse | 25 | D6 |
| Lobster | 26 | C4 |
| Typhoon | (see 24) | |

### 🍸 DRINK
| | | |
|---|---|---|
| Cameo at the Viceroy | 27 | C4 |
| Father's Office | 28 | B2 |
| Novel Café | 29 | D6 |
| Ye Olde King's Head | 30 | B4 |

### ★ PLAY
| | | |
|---|---|---|
| Harvelle's | 31 | C4 |
| McCabe's Guitar Shop | 32 | G2 |

Please see over for map

## SEE

### BERGAMOT STATION

☎ 310-453-7535; www.bergamot station.com; 2525 Michigan Ave; admission free; ☾ 10am-6pm Tue-Fri, 11am-5:30pm Sat; 🚌 BBB 5; Ⓟ

One of LA's best-known art nodes, this one-time trolley stop now houses 35 contemporary art galleries, the **Santa Monica Museum of Art** ( ☎ 310-586-6488; www.smmoa .org; ☾ 11am-6pm), a café, and plenty of free parking on its 8-acre, campus-style complex. Stop by the museum for cutting-edge exhibits, a map and a look at the orange-tiered shelves of Gracie, an artistically inclined, non-traditional gift shop.

### PALISADES PARK

☎ 800-544-5319; southern terminus at cnr Colorado Blvd & Ocean Ave; admission free; ☾ 5am-midnight; 🚌 BBB 1; 🚻

Perhaps it's appropriate that Route 66, America's most romanticized by-way, ends at this gorgeous cliffside park perched dramatically on the edge of the continent. Just pretend you don't see all the beggars. Stretching 1.5 miles north from the pier, this palm-dotted greenway is tops with joggers and people-watchers. For turn-of-the-20th-century thrills, grab a key to the tower-bound **Camera Obscura** (Senior Recreation Center, 1450 Ocean Ave) for a few spins of an old captain's wheel that gives inverted-mirror views of the park below.

Late afternoon in Palisades Park

### ☀ SANTA MONICA PIER & PACIFIC PARK

☎ 310-458-8900; www.santamonica
pier.org; cnr Colorado & Ocean Aves;
admission free; 🚌 BBB 1; ♿
Here since 1909, this landmark
pier is worth a quick visit – preferably during the day. Wander past
an indoor carousel, an arcade,
several restaurants, myriad vendors and oodles of other tourists.
Near the pier's end, check out
a nifty black-and-white photo
exhibit of the pier's history. **Pacific
Park** ( ☎ 310-260-8744; www.pacpark
.com) is the pay-as-you go amuse-
ment park. Pay $2 for seven

rotations on the Pacific Wheel,
the world's only solar-powered
Ferris wheel.

### ☀ SANTA MONICA PIER AQUARIUM

☎ 310-393-6149; www.healthebay
.org; 1600 Ocean Front Walk; admission
adult/under 12yr $5/free; 🕑 2-5pm Tue-
Fri, 12:30-5pm Sat & Sun, extended hours
Jun-Aug; 🚌 BBB 2; ♿
Peer under the pier – just below
the carousel – for Heal the Bay's
kid-friendly touch tanks crawl-
ing with critters and crustaceans
scooped from the bay. For a
fin-filled frenzy, stop by the shark

Solar-powered fun at Pacific Park

tanks at 3:30pm Sunday for feedings of these multifanged beasts.

### SANTA MONICA STATE BEACH

☎ 310-458-8411; www.smgov.net; admission free; 🚌 BBB 1; ♿

There are endless ways to play on the 3.5-mile blanket of strand stretching from Venice Beach in the south to Will Rogers State Beach in the north. If lying out isn't your thing, stop by **Perry's Café** (930 & 1200 Pacific Coast Hwy, 2400 & 2600 Ocean Front Walk) for skate, bike and board rentals. A section of the South Bay Bicycle Trail runs along the beach – pick it up under the pier. To reserve time on a **beach volley ball court** ( ☎ 310-458-8300), call and confirm applicable fees. For cerebral pursuits, settle in at a first-come first-served chess table at Chess Park, just south of the pier. As of October 2006, smoking is no longer permitted on Santa Monica beaches.

# 🛍 SHOP

### BABYSTYLE *Maternity & Baby*

☎ 310-434-9590; www.babystyle.com; 1324 Montana Ave; 🕙 10am-6pm Sun-Fri, to 7pm Sat; 🚌 BBB 3; ♿

The chicest babies in town kick their strollers toward the bright colors and cool fashions of Babystyle, cruising the stroller ramp into a wide selection of clothes

Smoke-free Santa Monica State Beach

and accessories perfect for every stage of mother- and babyhood. The tees for tots – 'Preschool is cool' – are impossibly cute.

### BLACK + BLUE *Men's Clothing*

☎ 310-664-9400; 2711 Main St; 🕙 11am-7pm Mon-Sat, to 6pm Sun; 🚌 BBB 1, Tide Shuttle

Within the spare, rockin' walls of Black + Blue, fashion-forward fellas get their moment with the hottest labels and accessories in town – Theory, Stitches and Juicy Men plus a few homegrown faves like K&J shirts and Travis Walker rings.

### 🏠 BLONDE LA *Women's Clothing*
☎ 310-396-9113; www.blondela.com;
2430 Main St; ⏰ 11am-7pm Mon-Sat, to
6pm Sun; 🚌 BBB 1

Highlight your beach-chic roots
at this bright and sassy boutique
where the upbeat staff are ready
to dress your inner blonde with
the latest hoodies, camis, dresses
and denims.

### 🏠 HEAR MUSIC *Music*
☎ 310-319-9527; 1429 Third St
Promenade; ⏰ 9am-11pm Sun-Thu, to
midnight Fri & Sat; 🚌 BBB 4

The CD racks at most Starbucks
coffeeshops are nothing more
than precaffeine distractions. But
not at Hear Music, one of four
music retail stores in the US owned
by Starbucks where music comes
first, coffee second. Grab a latte,
peruse the rows of CDs or digital
catalog (more than a million songs
available), pick your faves, then
grab a seat at the Music Media Bar,
burn a custom mix, and embrace
the Starbucks lifestyle.

### 🏠 HORIZONS WEST *Surf Shop*
☎ 310-392-1122; 2011 Main St;
⏰ 10am-7pm Mon-Sat, 11am-6pm Sun,
closing times may be later, surf dependent; 🚌 BBB1

The sun won't be setting on Horizons West in the immediate future. This landmark surf shop was
granted a temporary reprieve from

demolition after neighbors rallied
the Santa Monica Landmarks
Commission. Sharing a roof with
tiny Zephyr skateboard shop, this
scruffy corner was the hangout for
the 1970s surfers and skate-rats
chronicled in the movies *Lords of
Dogtown* and *Dogtown & Z-boys*.
Inside, rent a board for $10 an
hour or browse the boardshorts,
flip-flops and beachy tees packing
the tiki-themed rooms.

### 🏠 PUZZLE ZOO *Toys*
☎ 310-393-9201; www.puzzlezoo
.com; 1413 Third St Promenade; 🚌 BBB
1,7,8; ♿

Those searching galaxy-wide for
the caped Lando Calrissian action
figure, look no more. Puzzle Zoo
stocks every imaginable Star Wars
figurine this side of Endor. For
non–Star Wars fans and kids, there
are hundreds of puzzles, board
games and toys jockeying for
space on scruffy, floor-to-ceiling
shelves.

### 🏠 UNDEFEATED *Specialty
Sneakers*
☎ 310-399-4195; www.undftd.com;
2654B Main St; 🚌 BBB 1

Sneaker lovers camp outside
this pint-sized store for the latest
'Outside the Box' styles from Nike,
Converse, Vans and Adidas, each
pair specially selected from the
manufacturer by the manager.

Magic and imagination at Whimsic Alley

Word spreads on the internet, and voila, sidewalk campouts. Also in **Mid-City** ( ☎ 323-937-6077; 112½ S La Brea Ave; ⏰ 11am-7pm Mon-Sat, 10am-4pm Sun).

🏠 **WHIMSIC ALLEY** *Boutique for Muggles & Wizards*
☎ 310-453-2370; www.whimsicalley.com; 2717½ Wilshire Blvd; ⏰ 11am-5pm Wed-Sun; 🚌 BBB 2; ♿
Muggles love this magical little store at 2717½, where Harry Potter and friends seem to wait just one portkey away. Superbly designed to invoke visions of Diagon Alley, you can flip through Hogwarts sweaters and capes at Haber & Dasher, find your favorite wand at Phoenix Wands, or just poke around nooks overflowing with Harry Potter memorabilia and literature on piratology, dragons and wandmaking.

# 🍴 EAT

🍴 **CAFÉ MONTANA**
*Californian*                                    $$
☎ 310-829-3990; www.montanave.com/cafemontana; 1534 Montana Ave; ⏰ 8am-3pm & 5:30-10pm; 🚌 BBB 3
Café Montana is an oh-so-LA café – where the chic elite nibble fresh pastries and Chinese chicken salad in a sparkling glass box. Don't be surprised to see Steven Spielberg, Tim Robbins or Susan Sarandon showing up for a noon-time nosh.

**Keith Gear**

*Surfer, teacher and dog-bed designer*

**How long have you been surfing in LA?** Twenty years. **Any beaches better for new surfers?** Malibu is ideal, but the locals can be feisty; stick close to the pier. Or go a few miles south on the PCH and look for GLADSTONES-4-FISH on the cliff, where Sunset meets the sunset. **Where can newbies rent surf equipment?** Horizons West (p100) in Santa Monica. **Any tips on etiquette?** Local surfers have a Clint Eastwood vibe out in the water. Don't be a kook by trying to catch someone else's wave if they're coming up behind you. Pull back and let them enjoy the ride. Also, try to observe a 4ft distance when the water is crowded. **You hike too. Any recommendations?** I sometimes lead groups from the Santa Monica Youth Hostel on the Temescal Canyon hike (boxed text, p55). When you get to the top there's a great sweeping view of Santa Monica. You can see downtown on a clear day.

Build your own burger at the Counter

## 🍴 COUNTER
*Hamburgers*                                    $

☎ 310-399-8383; www.thecounter
burger.com; 2901 Ocean Park Blvd, Ste
102; ⏱ 11am-10pm Mon-Thu, to 11pm
Fri & Sat, noon-9pm Sun; 🚌 BBB 8; ♿

Grab a clipboard and minipencil,
it's burger-building time at this
bright and cheery corner hotspot
that's best avoided by the indeci-
sive. From the four meat choices to
the 10 cheeses, 27 toppings (avocado, pepperocini and fried egg!)
and 17 sauces, it's all up to you.
Tasty fries are great for sharing.

## 🍴 EL CHOLO *Mexican*            $$

☎ 310-899-1106; www.elcholo.com;
1025 Wilshire Blvd; ⏱ 11am-10pm
Mon-Thu, to 11pm Fri & Sat, to 9pm Sun;
🚌 BBB2; ♿

Happy hipsters, hungry families
and rowdy birthday parties compete for tables at this festive two-
story adobe landmark. A handful
grumble that the food is so-so, but
the blue-corn chicken enchiladas,
potent margaritas and a buzzing
lounge keep most everyone coming back for more.

NEIGHBORHOODS

SANTA MONICA

### 🍴 HUMP Sushi $$$-$$$$

☎ 310-313-0977; www.thehump.biz;
3221 Donald Douglas Loop S, 3rd fl;
🕑 noon-2pm Tue-Fri, 6-10pm Sun-Thu,
to 10:30pm Fri & Sat; 🚌 BBB 14
Romance runs high behind the
bamboo-accented windows at
this tiny but superb rooftop sushi
bar with stellar views of private
planes soaring off to the great un-
known. The Hump – an aviators'
nickname for the Himalayas –

is perched on the 3rd floor of the
Santa Monica Airport building just
above bustling **Typhoon** (3221 Donald
Douglas Loop S, 2nd fl), where the pan-
Asian specialties menu includes
crickets.

### 🍴 LIBRARY ALEHOUSE
Gastropub $$-$$$
☎ 310-314-4855; www.libraryalehouse
.com; 2911 Main St; 🕑 11:30am-
midnight; 🚌 BBB 1

---

## WORTH THE TRIP: MALIBU

Everyone needs a little Malibu. And lucky for you, 30 miles of surf, sunshine and sun-dappled
mountains are only a tankful of gas away. Driving north on the Pacific Coast Hwy (PCH), the
recently reopened **Getty Villa** ( ☎ 310-440-7300; www.getty.edu/visit; 17985 PCH; admission free, reservations required; 🅿 ) awaits on the right with an impressive collection of Greek
and Roman antiquities. Parking costs $8. Next up is freewheeling Topanga, where the **Inn
of the Seventh Ray** ( ☎ 310-455-1311; www.innoftheseventhray.com; 128 Old Topanga
Canyon Rd) serves local seafood and organic dishes with new-age flair.

Cars and towel-draped surfers line the road at popular **Surfrider Beach** near the Malibu
pier. Just west is the museum at the 1930s **Adamson House** ( ☎ 310-456-8432; www.adam
sonhouse.org; 23200 PCH; tour adult/concession $5/2; 🕑 11am-2pm Wed-Sat), where exhib-
its highlight the history of the quirky Malibu Colony. Primo bird-watching awaits next door at
Malibu Lagoon State Beach. A sandy wander west leads past exclusive beachfront property –
don't fear the chain-link fence on the beach! The sand is private only to the mean high-tide line.
Back in the car, the next temptation is the terrace at **Geoffrey's** ( ☎ 310-457-1519; www
.geoffreysmalibu.com; 27400 PCH), where stylistas sip mimosas and nibble salad by the sea.

For elevated views, follow Heathercliff Rd to Dume Rd for the panorama from **Point
Dume State Preserve**, the western terminus of the Santa Monica Bay and perfect for
whale-watching. Sweet beaches roll up next, with the wide shores of **Zuma Beach County
Park** up first. Then on to the rocky coast of **El Matador State Beach** and the critter-
filled tidepools of **Leo Carillo State Beach**. Not far past the Malibu line, **Neptune's Net**
( ☎ 310-457-3095; www.neptunesnet.com; 42505 PCH) catches Range Rovers, road bikes
and rad choppers with fried-shrimp-and-beer hospitality on inviting wooden porches. A bit
further are sycamore-lined mountain trails and seaside views of frolicking seals at lustrous
**Point Mugu State Park**.

Ocean views and ocean fare at Lobster

Locals gather for the food as much as the beer within the wood-paneled walls of Main St's friendliest gastropub. Ahi burgers, fish tacos and hearty salads sate the 30-something postwork regulars while 29 hand-crafted microbrews keep 'em hanging around 'til midnight.

**LOBSTER** *Seafood* $$$
☎ 310-458-9294; www.thelobster.com; 1602 Ocean Ave; ⏰ 11:30am-10:30pm Sun-Thu, 11.30am-11pm Fri & Sat; 🚌 BBB 1; ♿
Chef Allyson Thurber crafts lobster and seafood specials as stunning as the oceanfront views at this

**GREEN MACHINE**

For the nature-minded, try the free **ParkLink Shuttle** ( ☎ 888-734-2323; www.parklinkshuttle.com) service that runs between Malibu's coastal and mountain parks, provided by the Mountains Conservation & Recreation Authority in conjunction with state and local parks. Start your ramble at one park then return on a clean diesel shuttle or just use it to loop to scenic viewpoints. Bikes and wheelchairs are welcome, but not pets. Maps and outdoor-event calendars are available onboard. Shuttles run weekends only year-round, 8am to 5pm fall through spring and 8am to 8pm in summer.

The very Novel Café

lively pierside perch. Tables are tight and the noise levels high, but that's de rigueur at the beach.

# 🍸 DRINK

## 🍸 CAMEO AT THE VICEROY
*Lounge*

☎ 310-451-8711; www.viceroy
santamonica.com; 1819 Ocean Ave;
🕒 10:30am-1am; 🚌 MTA 33

This is where 007 Bond girls lounge between bouts of international espionage. Cabanas, sexy lighting and arm-candy galore – slink over to this simmering shoebox off the lobby of the Viceroy Hotel and release your inner superspy.

## 🍸 FATHER'S OFFICE
*Gastropub*

☎ 310-393-2337; 1018 Montana Ave;
🕒 bar from 3pm, kitchen from 5pm;
🚌 BBB 3

Everybody knows your name, or they soon will, at this loud, elbow-to-elbow, almost-an-icon watering hole where barkeeps skillfully explain 30+ beers on tap. Just don't ask for substitutions on the decadent burger: eat it as is or not at all, it's one of the best in town.

### ☎ NOVEL CAFÉ *Coffeeshop*
☎ 310-396-8566; www.novelcafe.com; 212 Pier Ave; ⏲ 7am-1am Mon-Fri, 8am-1am Sat, 8am-midnight Sun; 🚌 BBB 1; Ⓥ

With numerous nooks, walls of books, and a loiterer-friendly feel, Novel Café is a low-key indie coffeeshop (and used bookstore) favored by writers, beach bums and tired Main St shoppers looking for an attitude-free caffeine infusion.

### ☎ YE OLDE KING'S HEAD
*British Pub*
☎ 310-451-1402; 116 S Santa Monica Blvd; ⏲ 11am-1.30am, kitchen closes 10pm Mon-Thu & midnight Fri-Sun; 🚌 BBB 1

A mixed-age crew frequents this 30-year expat fave that's fun for the colonists too. Expect dartboards, football (the other kind)

and lots of ales on tap. A slim bar menu includes hefty fish'n'chips.

## ⭐ PLAY

### ❑ HARVELLE'S *Live Music*
☎ 310-395-1676; www.harvelles.com; 1432 4th St; ⏲ 8pm-2am; 🚌 BBB 2

Follow the sexy red glow and jazz-infused beats to cozy Harvelle's, way too cool for its 4th St, garage-adjacent digs. Sunday night's Pure Unadulterated Soul is rumored to be unforgettable.

### ❑ MCCABE'S GUITAR SHOP
*Live Music*
☎ 310-828-4497; www.mccabes.com; 3101 Pico Blvd; shows $8-20; ⏲ 10am-10pm Mon-Thu, 10am-6pm Fri & Sat, noon-5pm Sun; 🚌 BBB 13

Fast approaching its 50th birthday, this is the little guitar shop that could – hosting some of the best small-venue shows around in its no-frills but still cosy back room. Past bluegrass, folk and indie standouts include Ralph Stanley, Lucinda Williams and Gillian Welch and David Rawlings.

# >VENICE

Venice is just plain cool. In fact, its coolness threatens to eat it alive and spit it back out as Santa Monica. In the century following entrepreneur Abbot Kinney's original vision of a cultural 'Venice of America,' the reality of his dream has been slightly askew. Over the years the neighborhood has attracted artists, visionaries and dreamers to its canals and crooked streets as well as its fair share of deadbeats, drunkards and trouble-makers.

Ocean Front Walk exemplifies the kooky side of the unfettered dream – vendors, muscle men and unabashed performers bumping elbows for attention. It's a little bit crazy and a whole lot of fun. Abbot Kinney Blvd on the other hand, with its independent boutiques and customer-centric eateries, boasts the best of focused indie spirit. No chains, franchises or green-smocked baristas on this hard-charging boulevard. Both approaches make Venice what it is. Even if you never visit, it's nice to know it exists.

## VENICE

# SEE
## LA LOUVER
☎ 310-822-4955; www.lalouver.com; 45 N Venice Blvd; admission free; ⏲ 10am-6pm Tue-Sat; 🚌 MTA 33, 333

Inside the sleek, cool walls of LA Louver, it's easy to forget the adjacent Venice Beach kookiness. Exhibits in this compact two-story gallery rotate every few months but expect an array of contemporary artists from LA up-and-comers to established international names.

## OCEAN FRONT WALK
Venice Pier to Rose Ave; ⏲ 24hr; 🚌 MTA 33, 333, BBB 2

Known locally as the Venice Boardwalk, this can't-miss parade of hustlers, freaks, artists and exhibition-ists will have you either thanking your lucky stars for your office job or plotting your imminent escape from drudgery. Looking to shop? Cheap sunglasses, Bob Marley tees, beachy photographs and sarongs are representative fare. Personal makeover? Body piercers, tattoo artists, open-air masseuses and hair-braiders are happy to help. Hungry? Sausages, funnel cakes and burgers abound.

## VENICE CANAL WALK
⏲ 24hr; 🚌 MTA 33, 333

Just northeast of the Washington Blvd and Pacific Ave intersection, it's a step through the looking glass from the traffic-clogged roar of Washington Blvd to the bougainvillea-lined bungalows bordering Venice's once-plentiful canals. Wandering the narrow, impossibly cute bridges and walkways, it's tough to keep envy in check as dog-walkers, surfers and grandmas pass by, enjoying their tranquil patch of paradise.

# SHOP
## BRICK LANE Men's & Women's Clothing
☎ 310-392-2525; www.bricklaneuk.com; 1132 Abbot Kinney Blvd; ⏲ 10am-6pm Tue-Sat, noon-6pm Sun & Mon; 🚌 MTA 33, 333

No time for London this year? Pop over to Brick Lane, just past

### ART IS ALL AROUND US
Who needs galleries when you've got outdoor art? Just ask Jonathan Borofsky's 30ft sad-faced ballerina clown looming over Long's Drug at the corner of Main St and Rose Ave. Or walk one block south to ponder Claes Oldenburg and Coosje van Bruggen's massive binoculars, flanking the Frank Gehry–designed Chiat/Day building. As for murals, Venice has a plethora, so be sure to look up while you walk. Along Ocean Front Walk, check out Rip Cronk's *Venice Reconstituted* and *Homage to a Starry Night*, a tribute to Vincent Van Gogh.

the red phone booth, to dress as if you'd been there. A mix of new and stylishly familiar (Issa, Ted Baker, Ben Sherman) – whatever It Is you fancy, the friendly staff in this upscale British bungalow will fix you up with just the right London look.

### ◻ EQUATOR BOOKS *Books*
☎ 310-399-5544; www.equatorbooks .com; 1103 Abbot Kinney Blvd; 🕙 11am-10pm Tue-Thu, to 11pm Fri & Sat, to 5pm Sun; 🚍 MTA 33, 333
Locals ride their bikes into this garage-style indie bookstore, open since 2004. The right side of the shop features tall shelves of out-of-print and collectable books running the gamut from Alex Haley's *Roots* to Umberto Eco's *Travels with Mayan Realities*. On the left you'll find new books focusing on surf and skate, music and, well, circus freaks and bullfighting. Art exhibits are displayed in the center.

### ◻ FIREFLY *Women's Clothing & Gifts*
☎ 310-450-6288; www.shopfirefly.com; 1413 Abbot Kinney Blvd; 🕙 11am-7pm Mon-Sat, to 5pm Sun; 🚍 33, 333
You'll feel like Skipper hanging at Barbie's Awesome Beach Bungalow at this peppy little shop. Gifty candles, journals and cookbooks chatter up front while chic beach dresses and tees giggle in back.

Too hot to trot on the Venice Boardwalk

Careful though, naughty cards are stacked just across from adorable toddler toys.

### ◻ JUST TANTAU *Gifts*
☎ 310-392-4646; 1353 Abbot Kinney Blvd; 🕙 10am-9pm; 🚍 MA 33, 333
Everything a gift store should be – fun, happy to see you, and stocked with one-of-a-kind gifts. Worth a closer look: handmade ornaments, naughty checkbook covers, Venice canal prints, and playful fine jewelry. The bracelets made from old-fashioned typewriter keys are a kick. Guys can gain points with a 'just-because-I-wanted-to' perfect gift for that special gal.

## SMALL WORLD BOOKS
*Books*

☎ 310-399-2360; www.smallworld
books.com; 1407 Ocean Front Walk;
🕐 10am-8pm; 🚌 MTA 33, 333, BBB 2

Look closely or you'll miss Small
World Books, tucked beside the
overflowing patio of Sidewalk Café.
Small but jam-packed – with requi-
site cat – this welcoming indie has
an eclectic inventory reflecting the
interests of Venice denizens: film,
Eastern philosophy and travel, to
name just a few. Vampires will appreciate the dark spookiness of the
crammed mystery annex. Plenty of
beach reads too.

## STRANGE INVISIBLE
PERFUMES *Perfumes & Lotions*

☎ 310-314-1505; www.siperfumes.com;
1138 Abbot Kinney Blvd; 🕐 11am-7pm
Tue-Sat, noon-6pm Sun; 🚌 MTA 33, 333

Walk-ins welcome at this upscale
but accessible perfumery where
fragrances are personally crafted.
Discover that perfect soulful scent
at the consultation bar or wander
past cool, lavender-toned walls for
an equally fascinating array of natu-
rally fragranced cleansers, scrubs
and creams that will leave you feeling neither strange nor invisible.

## SURFING COWBOYS
*Furniture*

☎ 310-450-4891; www.surfing
cowboys.com; 1624 Abbot Kinney Blvd;

🕐 11am-7pm Tue-Sat, 11am-6pm Sun;
🚌 MTA 33, 333

Giddyup bro. Bring your lasso
and your wallet to the funkiest
purveyor of midcentury furniture
and surf memorabilia this side of,
well, anywhere. Filled with vintage
surfboards and skateboards, retro
but comfy couches, historic beach
photos and gently worn cowboy
boots, it has friendly staff who are
happy to show you around the
eclectic mix. Just don't hem and
haw too long; turnover is quick.

# 🍴 EAT

## 🍴 ABBOT'S PIZZA *Pizza* $

☎ 310-399-1171; 1407 Abbot Kinney
Blvd; 🕐 11am-11pm; 🚌 MTA 33, 333;
Ⓥ 👶

Surfers have savored Abbot's
Pizza gourmet slices for years but
word of the crispy-crusted specialties – tequila-lime chicken, wild
mushroom – has spread far beyond
the flip-flop crowd that consistent-
ly fills the handful of tables at this
elevator-sized hotspot. Midafter-
noon, ask for a fresh-from-the-oven
slice – heat lamps spoil the fun.

## 🍴 JODY MARONI'S SAUSAGE
KINGDOM *Sausages* $

☎ 310-822-5639; www.jodymaroni
.com; 2011 Ocean Front Walk; 🕐 10am-
sunset; 🚌 MTA 33, 333, BBB 2; 👶 👶

It's the free samples that get
you. Spicy hot Italian, chicken

Comrades commune at Mao's Kitchen

Andouille, Louisiana hot links: once you've had a taste of one of Jody's gourmet sausages, it's near impossible not to order the whole onions and peppers shebang. Serving 'em up on fresh-baked rolls since 1979, Jody's is the place to refuel after a long day of Ocean Front Walk gawking.

### JOE'S *Cal-French* $$$-$$$$
☎ 310-399-5811; www.joesrestaurant .com; 1023 Abbot Kinney Blvd; ⊙ noon-2:30pm Tue-Fri, 11am-2:30pm Sat & Sun, 6-10pm Sun & Tue-Thu, 6-11pm Fri & Sat; 🚌 MTA 33, 333
With its superb Cal-French cuisine, thoughtfully prepared prix fixe menus, top-notch service and a warm ambience, dining at Joe's

is like receiving a gift prepared especially for you. The seafood – try the grilled shrimp on saffron risotto – is especially exquisite. Upscale but not pretentious, Joe's is a perfect lunch stop after a morning of Abbot Kinney shopping.

### MAO'S KITCHEN
*Chinese* $-$$
☎ 310-581-8305; www.maoskitchen .com; 1512 Pacific Ave; ⊙ 11:30am-10:30pm Sun-Thu, to 3am Fri & Sat; 🚌 MTA 33, 333; Ⓥ ♿
'Serve the People!' is the motto at red-bricked Mao's, so settle in with easy-going comrades at a communal table – capitalists permitted to sit alone – and choose

from Chinese favorites made with a lighter, SoCal flair. Proles most often request the orange chicken. The small salad is just $1.

### PRIMITIVO WINE BISTRO
*Tapas* $$-$$$

☎ 310-396-5353; www.primitivowine bistro.com; 1025 Abbot Kinney Blvd; 🕑 noon-2:30pm Mon-Fri, 5:30pm-midnight Fri-Sat, 5:30-10:30pm Sun-Thu; 🚍 MTA 33, 333

Primitivo will bring your sexy back. From the sensuous Mediterranean designs to the luscious hot tapas to the thoughtfully paired wines, this rustic wine bar inspires a sultry mood perfect for a romantic rendezvous. Sautéed tiger shrimp,

seared scallops and the bacon-wrapped dates may keep you from ever going home.

### THREE SQUARE BAKERY & CAFÉ *Bakery* $

☎ 310-399-6504; 1121 Abbot Kinney Blvd; 🕑 7am-6pm; 🚍 MTA 33, 333

The decor may be minimalist chic, but the scones, croissants, tarts and cheesy pretzels jostling for space under this new bakery's happenin' glass counter are anything but. Strong Julian Meinl coffee, an array of fresh breads and gourmet sandwiches round out the everything-looks-scrumptious menu. Try the chocolate lavender torte.

Easy-going drinks at the Otheroom

# 🍸 DRINK

## 🍸 ABBOT'S HABIT *Café*

☎ 310-399-7334; 1401 Abbot Kinney Blvd; ⏱ 6am-10pm Sun-Thu, to 11pm Fri & Sat; 🚌 MTA 33, 333

With its crunchy, unwashed vibe – messenger bags, dreadlocked hippies, '80s indie classics on the airwaves – scruffy Abbot's Habit feels more Colorado mountain town than shiny LA surf city. But then you see the flip-flops, dude, and it all seems right. The coffee's strong, the pastries are fresh and the patio's made for loitering. Check it out, bro.

## 🍸 ON THE WATERFRONT CAFÉ *Café*

☎ 310-392-0322; www.waterfrontcafe .com; 205 Ocean Front Walk; 🚌 MTA 33, 333

For a little German-style conviviality, oom-pah-pah your way over to the lively patios at On the Waterfront Cafe, where a boisterous international crew guzzles pitchers of Bitburger and Erdinger. Lots of pub grub and a few Germanic specialties – potato pancakes, bratwurst, Swiss dried beef – keep the boardwalk-adjacent revelers going all day long.

## 🍸 OTHEROOM *Bar*

☎ 310-396-6230; 1201 Abbot Kinney Blvd; ⏱ 5pm-2am; 🚌 MTA 33, 333

With its loungey red-brick and candlelight style, the two-year-old Otheroom looks like any Hollywood hipster haven. The difference? A refreshing lack of attitude – just folks kickin' back and perusing a chalkboard beer list. And with more than 70 to choose from, that's gonna take some time. No food is served but deliveries to your table from outside are welcome.

# >SOUTH BAY

Although the three beach towns south of LAX – Manhattan, Hermosa and Redondo – aren't far geographically from the rest of LA, the mindset's a whole 'nuther story. Simply put, people are more kicked back. Maybe it's waking to the sight of sparkling surf, the caress of cool ocean breezes or the sound of volleyball players prepping for another round. Or maybe it's all the fresh air. Regular exercise is assumed, and outdoor exercise preferred. Bikers, runners, swimmers – the place is one giant triathlon in training.

A few other things are also de rigueur – summer beach festivals, outdoor dining, Rock'n Fish apple martinis, and flip-flops for every occasion. Yes, the beaches have their share of drunken frats boys, vapid reality stars and pretty-on-the-outside scenesters, but there are quieter, more sublime views to be had. Just follow the Pacific Coast Hwy south until you hit Palos Verdes Dr and follow its stunning shoreline views around the peninsula's perimeter.

## SOUTH BAY

### 👁 SEE
| | | |
|---|---|---|
| Fun Bunn's | 1 | A6 |
| Manhattan Beach | 2 | A6 |
| Roundhouse Aquarium | 3 | A6 |
| Sand Dune Park | 4 | A1 |

### 🏠 SHOP
| | | |
|---|---|---|
| Buster & Sullivan | 5 | B5 |
| John Post Gallery | 6 | B6 |
| Wright's | 7 | B6 |

### 🍴 EAT
| | | |
|---|---|---|
| Bluewater Grill | 8 | C6 |
| Martha's 22nd Street Grill | 9 | B4 |
| Petros Greek Cuisine & Lounge | 10 | B5 |
| Rock'n Fish | 11 | A6 |
| Uncle Bill's Pancake House | 12 | A5 |

### 🍸 DRINK
| | | |
|---|---|---|
| Ercole's | 13 | A6 |
| Fat Face Fenner's Fishack | 14 | B4 |
| Hennessey's Tavern | 15 | B4 |
| Patrick Malloy's | (see 14) | |
| Union Cattle Company | 16 | B4 |
| Zinc Lounge | 17 | B5 |

### ⭐ PLAY
| | | |
|---|---|---|
| Comedy & Magic Club | 18 | B4 |

# SEE

## MANHATTAN BEACH

**www.citymb.info; 🚍 MTA 126, 439; 🚶**
If Manhattan Beach had its own
magazine, it would surely be
called *Gorgeous Living*. Classy
beachside cottages, bougainvillea-
lined walk-streets, bustling sidewalk patios, friendly boutiques,
surfers silhouetted against the
setting sun, and babies who never
seem to cry – all within half a
mile of a portrait-worthy pier. It's
that impossibly perfect. Outdoor
enthusiasts should check out **Fun
Bunn's** ( ☎ 310-372-8500; 1116 Manhattan
Ave; 🕐 10am-5:30pm Wed-Mon), where
rentals include beach cruisers,
surfboards, in-line skates, wetsuits
and volleyballs.

## POINT VICENTE INTERPRETIVE CENTER

☎ 310-377-5370; 31501 Palos Verdes Dr
W, Rancho Palos Verdes; admission free;
🕐 10am-5pm; 🚍 MTA 126
Captain Ahab's no match for the
binocular-toting crowd at this
primo whale-watching spot. From
December to May the faithful
huddle early on terraced patios to
watch for migrating grays. Check
the chalkboard for daily counts.
If whales aren't your thing, savor
towering cliffside views or pop
inside for engaging displays on
local history and geography.

Sun, skin and socialising at the South Bay

### 🔵 ROUNDHOUSE AQUARIUM

☎ 310-379-8117; www.roundhouse aquarium.org; Manhattan Beach Pier, Manhattan Beach; donations $2; ⏱ 3pm-sunset Mon-Fri, 10am-sunset Sat & Sun; 🚌 MTA 126, 439

Kids crowd the touch tanks at this tiny pier's-end aquarium while their parents stare warily at the flickering fins in the 3500-gallon shark tank. Upstairs, smaller tanks hold an eclectic mix of local specimens including the clicking garibaldi and sarcastic fringehead – sometimes seen lurking barside at Zinc.

### 🔵 SAND DUNE PARK

www.citymb.info; 33rd & Bell Ave, Manhattan Beach; admission free; ⏱ 6am-9pm Apr-Oct, 6am-8pm Nov-Mar, dunes open 7:30am; 🚌 MTA 125, 439; 🚻

Kick off your flip-flops for an impromptu workout on these steep, 100ft sand dunes hidden on a residential block near the intersection of Rosecrans and Highland Aves. Who knows, you might just see a Laker working his quads too. Whether you run, walk or crawl, it's steeper than it looks.

### 🔵 WAYFARERS CHAPEL

☎ 310-377-1650; www.wayfarers chapel.org; 5755 Palos Verdes Dr S, Rancho Palos Verdes; admission free; ⏱ 8am-5pm; 🚌 MTA 226

Glass walls and redwood pillars comfort tired wayfarers at Lloyd Wright's stunning seaside sanctuary. Built in 1951, this hillside 'tree chapel' supports an active congregation sponsored by the all-welcoming Swedenborgian Church. Guests should wander the Colonnade for reflective ocean views. Brides should book early.

## 🛍 SHOP

### 🏠 BUSTER & SULLIVAN *Pets*

☎ 310-802-1410; www.busterand sullivan.com; 451 Manhattan Beach Blvd, Manhattan Beach; ⏱ 11am-7pm Mon-Thu, 10am-7pm Fri & Sat, 10am-6pm Sun; 🚌 MTA 126

There's no such thing as a bad dog at Buster & Sullivan. Argyle sweaters, candy-striped cabana beds and 'Chewy Vuitton' plush toys ensure you'll have the most stylish pooch in town. Basset hounds, pocket puggles, Great Danes – all are welcome at this high-end doggy boutique. Don't miss the biscuit bar.

### 🏠 JOHN POST GALLERY *Photographs*

☎ 310-376-6982; www.johnpost.com; 809 Manhattan Ave, Manhattan Beach; ⏱ noon-6pm Wed-Sun; 🚌 MTA 126

Photographer John Post captures South Bay landscapes like no other, and he's been at it for 31 years. Colorful, iconic shots of lonely lifeguard stands, blossoming walk-streets and SoCal sunsets

NEIGHBORHOODS

SOUTH BAY

Moving to the groove at Redondo

have made him a local darling. His pint-sized gallery is well stocked with prints, posters and panoramas – some of the shots taken during global travels.

### 📷 RIVIERA VILLAGE *Shopping District*
**www.rivieravillage.org; blocks surrounding Catalina Ave & Ave I, Redondo Beach; Ⓜ MTA 439**
Shoppers unite! Shake off the chains that bind you along the charming sidewalks of Riviera Village, where 150 boutiques, specialty stores, restaurants and

salons fill six bustling blocks, with nary a Gap nor B Dalton's in sight. From the beachy stylings of **Lisa Z** (1901 S Catalina Ave) to the Tommy Bahama flair of **Threads** (1907 S Catalina Ave) to the precious PJs of **Little Moon** (1813 S Catalina Ave), you'll find something you want to bring home. Post stroll, relax with a latte at laid-back, book-filled **Coffee Cartel** (1820 S Catalina, 102).

### 👕 WRIGHT'S *Women's Clothing*
**☎ 310-376-8553; 232 Manhattan Beach Blvd; 🕐 10am-7pm Mon-Fri, 9am-7pm Sat, 9am-6pm Sun; 🚌 MTA 126**
This cozy corner boutique proffers racks and stacks of high-end designer labels for the beach chic set – Velvet, Habit and Rozae Nichols to name a few. If you fancy some fashion for your favorite tot, **Baby Wright's** (1146 Highland Ave) is just a stroller push away, with Paul Frank, tiny lumberjack shirts, Naturino booties – it's all just simply adorable.

## 🍴 EAT

### 🍴 BLUEWATER GRILL
*Seafood*                          $$-$$$
**☎ 310-318-3474; www.bluewatergrill.com; 665 N Harbor Dr, Redondo Beach; 🕐 11:30am-10pm Mon-Thu, 11:30am-11pm Fri & Sat, 11am-10pm Sun; 🚌 MTA 439**
Step up to the oyster bar, order a dozen on the half shell then sit

back and watch the sun call it a day. For dinner, pick your fresh fish from the list then let the pros cook it any way you like. Garlic mashed potatoes and sautéed spinach (!) are can't-miss. The houseboat crowd slips in from the adjacent marina by 6:30pm for supercheap happy-hour prices.

### 🍴 MARTHA'S 22ND STREET GRILL *Breakfast* $

☎ 310-376-7786; 25 22nd St, Hermosa Beach; ⌚ 7am-3pm; 🚌 MTA 130, 439; ♿

Every table has an ocean view on the cheery umbrella'd patio just steps from the Strand. Martha's scrumptious scrambles, tasty wraps and addictive chicken cilantro soup keep locals rolling in by bike, blade and stroller. Don't worry, the waiting list moves fast.

### 🍴 PETROS GREEK CUISINE & LOUNGE *Greek* $$$

☎ 310-545-4100; www.petros restaurant.com; 451 Manhattan Beach Blvd, Manhattan Beach; ⌚ 11am-11pm Sun-Thu, 11am-midnight Fri & Sat; 🚌 MTA 126, 439

Petros – the place that launched a thousand positive reviews – may be new on the scene, but top-notch service, superb Greek specialties and a friendly, upscale vibe have made this charmer

**PIERSIDE PARTY**

Hermosa's pierside pedestrian promenade, Pier Ave, is one big party on weeknights and all day on weekends. It's a rowdy, early-20s crowd with revelers making their way between bars that include **Patrick Malloy's** ( ☎ 310-798-976250; Pier Ave) and **Fat Face Fenner's Fishack** ( ☎ 310-379-5550; 53 Pier Ave).

worthy of critics' kudos. Locals like it too. Grab a seat on the people-watching patio or lose your baseball cap for a dress-code-worthy experience indoors.

### 🍴 ROCK'N FISH *Seafood* $$-$$$

☎ 310-379-9900; www.rocknfishmb .com; 120 Manhattan Beach Blvd, Manhattan Beach; ⌚ 11:30am-10pm Sun-Wed, 11:30am-10:30pm Thu, 11:30am-11pm Fri-Sat; 🚌 MTA 126, 439

Sometimes it's about the blackened halibut, sometimes it's about the smokin' waitstaff, but it's always, always about the sour apple martini at sexy Rock'n Fish, just steps from the Manhattan Beach Pier. Part seafood restaurant, part upscale bar, this appropriately named hangout is an always-popular fallback. Great for group dinners or an early date, it's boisterous once the martini crowd flows in.

### 🍴 UNCLE BILL'S PANCAKE HOUSE *Pancakes* $

☎ 310-545-5177; 1305 N Highland Ave; ⏰ 6am-3pm Mon-Fri, 7am-3pm Sat & Sun; 🚌 MTA 126, 439; V ♿

Nothin' could be finer than a pancake in a diner known far and wide as Uncle Bill's. Grab a stool, grab a booth, or best yet grab a table on the sun-drenched patio. In season, the pumpkin spice pancakes are can't-miss. Omelets are darn good too. Tousled hipsters, tottering toddlers, gabbing girlfriends – everybody's here or on the way. Put your name on the clipboard, quick.

Fine dining at Uncle Bill's Pancake House

## 🍸 DRINK

### 🍸 ERCOLE'S *Bar*

☎ 310-372-1997; 1101 Manhattan Ave, Manhattan Beach; ⏰ 10am-2am; 🚌 MTA 126, 439

Check your attitude at the door at scruffy but lovable Ercole's – the South Bay's favorite dive since 1927. Old salts, pub crawlers, volleyball stars, wobbly co-eds – expect all to wander in. What's best? The $8 pitchers and Taco Tuesdays.

### 🍸 HENNESSEY'S TAVERN *Pub*

☎ 310-372-5759; www.hennesseys tavern.com; 8 Pier Ave, Hermosa Beach; ⏰ 7am-2am; 🚌 MTA 439

With a little luck o' the Irish, you'll nab a table on the bustling rooftop deck just in time for sun-set. Grab a Guinness and burger at this pier's-end pub – always fun but a smidge less rowdy than the frat-pack magnets crowding the rest of the pier.

### 🍸 UNION CATTLE COMPANY *Bar*

☎ 310-798-8227; www.unioncattle company.com; 1301 Manhattan Ave, Hermosa Beach; ⏰ 5pm-last call Mon-Wed, 5pm-2am Thu & Fri, 4pm-2am Sat, 4pm-11pm Sun; 🚌 MTA 439

Sometimes you wanna go to the beach, grab a cold brew, dance with your honey and…ride a mechanical bull. That's right, rowdy rustlers test their skills right in the center of the restaurant. Great for bachelorette parties, liquid birthdays, packs of singles and wannabe coastal cowboys.

## 🍸 ZINC LOUNGE *Bar*
☎ 310-546-4995; www.shadehotel.com; 1221 N Valley Dr, Manhattan Beach; 🕑 5-10pm Sun-Thu, 5-11pm Fri & Sat; 🚍 MTA 126, 439

Locals bring their A game to Shade Hotel's Zinc Lounge, the new kid in town everyone wants to befriend. Despite the club's sleek, deep-blue sheen – typically found in Hollywood hipster lounges – Zinc's well-dressed crowd is refreshingly relaxed and the bartenders friendly, albeit busy. The carefully considered small plate selections are popular – try the mini burgers – and serious imbibers should savor

the Shade Lemonade. Drink early; in consideration of hotel guests Zinc closes at 11pm.

## ⭐ PLAY
## ⭐ COMEDY & MAGIC CLUB
*Comedy & Magic*
☎ 310-372-1193; www.comedyand magicclub.com; 1018 Hermosa Ave, Hermosa Beach; 🚍 MTA 130, 439

Carlin, Foxworthy, Seinfeld – his puffy shirt is on display – have all paced the boards at Hermosa's Comedy & Magic Club. For big names, get here before 6pm to nab a good table and be ready to share your job or hometown with the ever-inquisitive opening acts. Always hot is Jay Leno, who tests out jokes most Sunday nights.

The pub at the end of the pier, Hennessey's Tavern

# >DOWNTOWN

Jostling past the umpteenth martini-sipping hipster, you finally reach the edge of the Standard's rooftop bar, pausing to savor twilight views of sleek skyscrapers, snow-capped mountains and sparkling city lights. Your first thought, despite the hassle? 'This is really cool.'

Others are now thinking the same. For years downtown was deserted after sunset when the briefcase brigade departed their Financial District fortresses. A few landmarks drew one-stop visitors but nobody spent the night. Then, in rapid succession, the Staples Center, the Standard Hotel and the Walt Disney Concert Hall opened their doors – dynamic developments igniting the downtown scene.

Today, contractors are busy flipping historic buildings into condos, new galleries are luring patrons, and trendy restaurants and bars are turning on the lights. The renaissance is still a work-in-progress – the Grand Ave development project looms and walking between nodes isn't recommended – but the energy's here. Like the Standard's rooftop bar, the bump-and-nudge vitality isn't to be missed.

## DOWNTOWN

### SEE
Avila Adobe .................... (see 3)
Cathedral of Our Lady
of the Angels ................... 1  E3
Chinese American
Museum ........................... 2  E3
El Pueblo Historical
Monument ....................... 3  E3
MOCA Geffen
Contemporary ................. 4  E4
Museum of
Contemporary Art .......... 5  D3
Richard J Riordan
Central Library ............... 6  D4
Sepulveda House .......... (see 3)
Walt Disney Concert
Hall ................................. 7  D3

### SHOP
California Market .......... 8  C5
Munky King ..................... 9  F2
New Mart ....................... 10  C5

### EAT
Ciudad ........................... 11  C3
Empress Pavilion .......... 12  F2
Grand Central Market ... 13  D4
Pete's Café & Bar .......... 14  D4
Philippe the Original .... 15  E3
R23 ................................ 16  F4
Water Grill .................... 17  D4
Yang Chow .................... 18  E2

### DRINK
Library Bar .................... 19  C4
Mountain Bar ............... 20  E2
Standard Rooftop Bar .. 21  C4

### PLAY
Dodger Stadium ............ 22  E1
Music Center of LA
County ........................... 23  D3
REDCAT ......................... 24  D3
Staples Center .............. 25  B5

Please see over for map

# ◉ SEE

## ◉ CALIFORNIA SCIENCE CENTER

☎ 323-724-3623; www.california sciencecenter.org; 700 State Dr, Exposition Park; admission free; ☽ 10am-5pm; 🚌 DASH F; Ⓟ ♿

From pedaling on a highwire bike to watching 50ft animatronic Tess maintain homeostasis, science here is state-of-the-art, highly interactive and loads of fun for families. The most low-tech exhibit inside the center's bright soaring walls may be the most interesting – baby chicks hatching in an incubator. To beat the fieldtrippers, visit after 1pm. Parking costs $6.

## ◉ CATHEDRAL OF OUR LADY OF THE ANGELS

☎ 213-680-5200; www.olacathedral .org; 555 W Temple St; admission free; ☽ 6:30am-6pm Mon-Fri, 9am-6pm Sat, 7am-6pm Sun; Ⓜ Civic Center; ♿ ♿

Architect Jose Rafael Moneo rewrote the cathedral builders' rulebook in 2002 with this flowing, freeform church complete with plazas, colonnades and a distinct disregard for right angles. His incorporation of regional styles and historic influences provides a welcoming air that's certainly helped by the gift store – famous locally for selling the cathedral's private-label chardonnay, cabernet and zin.

A woman with it all – Tess enthralls at the California Science Center

## CHINESE AMERICAN MUSEUM

☎ 213-485-8567; www.camla.com; 425 N Los Angeles St; suggested donation $3; ⏲ 10am-3pm Tue-Sun; Ⓜ Chinatown; ♿ ♿

This small but engaging museum spotlights the history of Chinese immigration in America – a history that parallels the current immigration debate like an eerily prescient fortune cookie. From America's dependence on cheap foreign labor to Congressional acts of Chinese exclusion, the newcomer's journey hasn't changed much in 100 years. In the adjacent exhibit hall, ponder the efficiency of the abacus in Sun Wing Wo's general store.

## EL PUEBLO HISTORICAL MONUMENT

☎ 213-628-1274; btwn Main & Alameda Sts; admission free; ⏲ visitor center 10am-3pm; Ⓜ Union Station; ♿

Nope, LA didn't spring from the head of Hollywood directors, it was a full-blown community a good 100 years before DW Griffith showed up. Grab a map at restored Firehouse No 1 (the Plaza Firehouse) then wander through narrow Olvera St's vibrant Mexican-themed stalls. For LA's oldest building, see **Avila Adobe** ( ☎ 213-628-1274; 125 Paseo de la Plaza; ⏲ 9am-4pm) then walk through the **Sepulveda House** ( ☎ 213-628-1274; 125 Paseo de la Plaza; ⏲ 9am-4pm) visitor center to see a restored 1800s-era kitchen and bedroom. The monument is situated east of I-101.

## MUSEUM OF CONTEMPORARY ART (MOCA)

☎ 213-626-6222; www.moca.org; 250 S Grand Ave; adult/student & senior/under 12yr $8/5/free; ⏲ 11am-5pm Mon & Fri, to 8pm Thu, to 6pm Sat & Sun; 🚌 DASH B; ♿

Architect Arata Osozaki built this conglomeration of cubes, pyramids and cylinders to house renowned collections of abstract expressionism, pop art, minimal-

El Pueblo presides

## THE HIPPEST BUILDING IN TOWN

Don't tell Walt Disney Concert Hall, but the **Richard J Riordan Central Library** ( ☎ 213-228-7000; www.lapl.org/Central; 630 W Fifth St; ☉ tours 12:30pm Mon-Fri, 11am & 2pm Sat, 2pm Sun), opened in 1926, is the most fascinating building in town. Yep, the library. The 64ft-high rotunda is the first big wow, its 42ft span highlighted by immense murals. Below, a 1-ton chandelier perches optimistically above the stark marble floor. In the 1993 Tom Bradley wing, escalators cascade below a soaring glass atrium, descending through four glass-walled floors filled with books. And Central has more than 2.1 million of those, not to mention a restaurant, gift store, free internet access and art exhibits. Tours led daily. Check it out. It's free.

ism and photography from the 5000-piece permanent collection. Same-day tickets are valid at Little Tokyo's **MOCA Geffen Contemporary** (152 N Central Ave). MOCA's satellite gallery at the Pacific Design Center (p64) is always free.

### ⊙ NATURAL HISTORY MUSEUM OF LOS ANGELES COUNTY

☎ 213-763-3466; www.nhm.org; 900 Exposition Blvd, Exposition Park; adult/ student, senior & 7-13yr/5-12yr/under 5yr $9/6.50/2/free, 1st Tue of month free; ☉ 9:30am-5pm Mon-Fri, 10am-5pm Sat & Sun; 🚌 DASH F; Ⓟ ♿ ♿

What's the most frightening *Night at the Museum* display at this warehouse of goodies? Is it the towering death match between T-rex and Triceratops in the great hall? Chest-thumping stuffed gorillas in the Hall of African Mammals? The 'human head' football games gruesomely described in the Hall of Ancient

Latin American? Perhaps it's the 200 shrieking 4th-graders tumbling off school buses at 9:35am. Decide for yourself but don't miss the Director's Hall, where a tiny portion of the museum's 33-million-piece collection is displayed based on the director's fancy. Parking $6.

### ⊙ WALT DISNEY CONCERT HALL

☎ 213-972-7211; www.musiccenter .org; 135 N Grand Ave; ☉ 10am-2pm, but confirm; 🚌 DASH A, DD, F; Ⓟ ♿

Architectural tours of Frank Gehry's steel-paneled masterpiece include a self-directed audio tour (adult/student, senior and group $12/10), public guided tour ($15) or an urban garden tour ($15). All are approximately 45 to 60 minutes. Times vary month to month due to performance schedules; call ☎ 323-850-2000 or see www .musiccenter.org/vtc/toursched .html. For general concert info check www.musiccenter.org /calendar or see the LA Philharmonic schedule at www.laphil .com. Parking costs $8 with validation. See also p14.

# 🛍 SHOP

## 👕 FASHION DISTRICT *Clothing*

☎ 213-488-1153; www.fashiondistrict .org; 🕑 10am-5pm, some stores closed Sun; 🚌 DASH D, E

Approximately 700 stores devoted to women's wear cluster on Los Angeles St between Olympic and Pico Blvds and on 11th St between Los Angeles and San Julian Sts; 360 men's wear stores and 169 children's wear fill surrounding blocks. On the last Friday of the month a few designer showrooms open briefly to unload samples and overstock at great prices. Sales take place from 9am to 3pm at **New Mart** ( ☎ 213-627-0671; 127 E 9th St) and **California Market** ( ☎ 213-630-3600; 110 E 9th St).

---

### SHUTTLE FORTH

Many downtown restaurants offer shuttle service to the Walt Disney Concert Hall and Dorothy Chandler Pavilion on performance nights, with shuttles running every 15 minutes. Call individual restaurants – Ciudad (right), R23 (p133) and Water Grill (p133) – to confirm service.

---

## 🧸 MUNKY KING

*Toys & Figurines*

☎ 213-620-8787; www.munkyking .com; 441 Gin Ling Way; 🕑 noon-7pm Mon-Tue, 11am-7pm Wed-Fri & Sun, 11am-8pm Sat; 🚇 Chinatown

Head to tiny Munky King where fanciful figurines – part toy, part art, part guilty pleasure – dot shelves like colorful candy confections. 'Individuality in the face of conformity,' is the official motto, and these individual-minded figurines clearly stick it to the man. Also in **Mid-City** (Map pp72–3, E2; ☎ 323-938-0091; 7308 Melrose Ave).

# 🍴 EAT

## 🍽 CIUDAD *Nuevo Latino* $$-$$$

☎ 213-486-5171; www.ciudad-la.com; 445 S Figueroa St; 🕑 11:30am-9pm Mon & Tue, 11:30am-10pm Wed & Thu, 11:30am-11pm Fri, 5-11pm Sat, 5-9pm Sun; 🚌 DASH A, DD, F, music center shuttle

With pan-Latin panache, the Two Hot Tamales of cable TV – Mary Sue Milliken and Susan Feniger – brighten the downtown corridor with empanadas, carnitas and other spicy specialties sprung from Spain and South America. Tuesday is 'Paella on the Patio' with the Spanish rice dish whipped up tableside on the ever-so-cute front patio. Mojitos are a must.

Fresh food galore at the Grand Central Market

## 🍴 EMPRESS PAVILION
*Chinese/Dim Sum* $$

☎ 213-617-9898; www.empress
pavilion.com; Bamboo Plaza, 988 N Hill
St; 🕙 10am-2:30pm Mon-Fri, 5:30-9pm
Mon-Thu, 5.30-9:30pm Fri, 9am-2:30pm
& 5-10pm Sat, 8:30am-2:30pm & 5-10pm
Sun; 🚌 DASH B, DD; 🅿 ♿
Great for groups, this Hong
Kong–style banquet hall has seat-
ing for a small village (500 people
to be exact). Delicacies fly off
the carts wheeled to your table
by a small army of servers. Off
the regular menu, seafood rarely
disappoints. There's a validated-
parking garage.

## 🍴 GRAND CENTRAL MARKET
*International* $

☎ 213-624-2378; www.grand
centralmarket.com; 317 S Broadway;
🕙 9am-6pm; 🚌 DASH DD; 🅿 🆅 ♿
You may have to muscle your way
to the counter for a taco at Ana
Maria's Mexican Food eatery, but
that's just part of the fun. Dating
from 1917, when Bunker Hill elite
would descend from their manors
via the Angel's Flight Railway (set
to reopen in 2007), the 38-stall
market maintains its street cred
with an eye-popping array of
fresh-food options. From apples to
chili peppers to kabobs, you want,
it they got. Somewhere. Parking
free with $10 validation.

## 🍴 PETE'S CAFÉ & BAR

*American* $$

☎ 213-617-1000; www.petescafe.com; 400 S Main St; 🕐 11:30am-2am Mon-Fri, 11am-2am Sat & Sun; Ⓜ Pershing Sq

Sparkling lights, glittering mirrors and towering mahogany walls project Victorian airs, but Norm-and-Cliff friendliness make this upbeat watering hole a mecca for chatty locals, postwork tipplers and those wanting a preshow bite. The menu spotlights salads, pastas and American standards. And check yourself out, girlfriend – the downstairs bathrooms have way-flattering mirrors.

## 🍴 PHILIPPE THE ORIGINAL

*American* $

☎ 213-628-3781; www.philippes.com; 1001 N Alameda St; 🕐 6am-10pm; 🚈 Union Station; 🚌 DASH B, DD; Ⓟ 🚼 Ⓥ

Celebrating its 100th birthday in 2008, Philippe the Original still hauls in hungry hordes with tasty French-dip sandwiches – created here decades ago by the original Philippe. With sawdust-covered floors, communal tables and nine-cent coffee, this landmark corner eatery a block north of Union Station remains a thriving cultural crossroads.

Plenty of choice at Philippe the Original

## SPORTS MINDED
### Baseball
**Los Angeles Angels of Anaheim** ( ☎ 714-940-2000; www.angelsbaseball.com) The 2002 World Series winners play at the Angels Stadium in Orange County.
**Los Angeles Dodgers** ( ☎ 866-363-4377; www.dodgers.com) Catch a major-league baseball game between April and September at Elysian Park's Dodger Stadium.

### Basketball
All teams play home games at downtown's **Staples Center** (1111 S Figueroa St).
**Los Angeles Clippers** (www.nba.com/clippers) Perennial underdogs but easier to snag tickets.
**Los Angeles Lakers** (www.nba.com/lakers) Kobe and gang play from October to April.
**LA Sparks** (www.wnba.com/sparks) The women's season follows the men's, running July to August.

### Soccer
**LA Galaxy** (www.lagalaxy.com) The arrival of David Beckham in 2007 may bend crowds toward Carson's Home Depot Center ( ☎ 310-630-2000; 18400 Avalon Blvd, Carson).

---

🍴 **R23** *Japanese* $$
☎ 213-687-7178; www.r23.com; 923 E 2nd St; 🕐 11:30am-2pm Mon-Fri, 5:30-10pm Mon-Sat; 🚌 DASH A, DD, music center shuttle
Frank Gehry–designed cardboard chairs are the seat du jour inside the minimalist redbrick interior of this popular sushi hideaway. At the sushi bar, exquisite daily specialties are masterfully prepared, but gracious chefs won't throw newbies to the curb for ordering California rolls.

🍴 **WATER GRILL** *Seafood* $$$$
☎ 213-891-0900; www.watergrill.com; 544 S Grand Ave; 🕐 11:30am-8:30pm Mon & Tue, 11:30am-9:30pm Wed-Fri, 5-9:30pm Sat, 4:30-8:30pm Sun, closing time is last reservation; 🚌 DASH B, C, DD, music center shuttle
Who needs the captain's table when impeccable service, fresh seafood and a warm, nautical ambience await in the heart of downtown? Locals linger over martinis at the raw bar while concertgoers savor preshow piscine specialties in the wood-beamed dining room.

### 🍴 YANG CHOW *Chinese* $-$$
☎ 213-625-0811; www.yangchow.com; 819 N Broadway; ⏰ 11:30am-9:45pm Sun-Thu, 11:30am-10:45pm Fri & Sat; Ⓜ Chinatown; ♿

All hail the slippery shrimp, the signature dish that's coaxed Angelenos to Chinatown for the last 30 years. Although outposts have opened in the Valley and Pasadena, the original downtown location, despite its coral-colored, somewhat uninspired decor, remains most popular.

## 🍸 DRINK

### 🍸 ANTIGUA CULTURAL COFFEE HOUSE *Coffeehouse*
☎ 323-539-2232; www.antigua coffeehouse.com; 4836 Huntington Dr S, El Sereno; ⏰ 7am-11pm Mon-Thu, to midnight Fri & Sat, to 10pm Sun; 🚌 MTA 78, 79; ♿

'From our plantation to yours' is the motto at this Mayan-themed coffeeshop where no one's a stranger for long. The coffee faithful loiter over magazines, listen to bands or just appreciate high-quality beans shipped directly from Antigua and roasted on site.

### 🍸 LIBRARY BAR *Bar*
☎ 213-614-0053; www.librarybarla.com; 630 W 6th St; ⏰ 3pm-2am Mon-Fri, 7pm-2am Sat & Sun; Ⓜ 7th/Metro Center

You won't be checking out books at this dark, elbow-to-elbow drinking pad where you may have to yell to be heard above the din. The book-lined bar with an East Coast vibe may be new to the scene but it's filling a void for the postwork thirsty looking for a low-attitude beer. Note, the entrance is on Hope St.

### 🍸 MOUNTAIN BAR *Bar*
☎ 213-625-7500; www.themountain bar.com; 473 Gin Ling Way; ⏰ 6.30pm-2am Tue-Sun; Ⓜ Chinatown

Poets and hipsters gather at this artsy Chinatown bar for a nightcap after gallery-hopping on nearby Chung King Rd. The Kool Aid–orange decor makes you feel like you're sitting inside a volcano.

### 🍸 STANDARD ROOFTOP BAR *Bar*
☎ 213-892-8080; www.thestandard .com; 55 S Flower St; admission after 7pm Fri & Sat $20; ⏰ noon-1:30am; Ⓜ 7th/Metro Center

Lawyers, scenesters and marketing execs mark territory beside space-pod cabanas and lounges at this rooftop oasis complete with pool. Once you find your way to the top – try escalator, elevator, stairs – the panoramic payoff is immense, with stunning views of skyscrapers backdropped by glowing mountains. Weekends, arrive before 7pm to beat the cover and the velvet rope.

Books and beer at bustling Library Bar

# ⭐ PLAY

## ⭐ MUSIC CENTER OF LA COUNTY *Performing Arts*

☎ theater 213-628-2772, dance 213-972-0711, opera 213-972-8001; www.musiccenter.org; 135 N Grand Ave; ticket prices vary; Ⓜ Civic Center; Ⓟ ♿

At this linchpin of the downtown performing arts scene, splashy musicals play to capacity at the Ahmanson Theatre, while the more intimate Mark Taper Forum premieres high-caliber plays. With Placido Domingo at the helm, the LA Opera has fine-tuned its repertory of classics by master composers, with performances at the Dorothy Chandler pavilion. Parking costs $8 in the evening.

## ⭐ REDCAT *Performing Arts*

☎ 213-237-2800; www.redcat.org; 631 W 2nd St; tickets $8-32, standard & member discounts; 🚌 DASH A, DD, F

The Roy and Edna Disney/Cal Arts Theater, tucked in the southwest corner of the Walt Disney Concert Hall complex, fosters new talent from around the world, presenting unique, sometimes challenging, performances in film, dance, theater, and art. Libations poured in sexy, shoeboxy **REDCAT Lounge** (🕐 9am-9pm Tue-Fri, noon-9pm Sat & Sun, & postshow).

# >BURBANK & UNIVERSAL CITY

For most of the 1800s, the San Fernando Valley was a barren plain held under two Spanish land grants. An enterprising dentist from New Hampshire, Dr David Burbank, purchased large portions of the tracts for a sheep ranch in the 1860s, later selling a $1 right-of-way to Southern Pacific Railroad, laying the tracks for people, commerce and increased property values. In 1915 German immigrant Carl Laemmle built a small studio on a sprawling chicken farm, called it Universal, and sold a few eggs to curious tourists. Warner Bros and Disney followed, and the region became the backbone of the entertainment industry, home of the hard work behind Hollywood's glamour. Today, tours and tapings at NBC/ Universal and Warner Bros studios provide a glimpse of this behind-the-scenes magic.

The surrounding neighborhoods – Toluca Lake, Studio City, Sherman Oaks – are filled with studio employees taking advantage of family-friendly streets. The attendant cookie-cutter sprawl, however, provides endless fodder for jokes about the 'The Valley.' But stay tuned; an influx of new restaurants, bars and condos suggests the trendiness tide could be turning.

## BURBANK & UNIVERSAL CITY

### ◉ SEE
Universal Studios ........... 1  D6
Warner Bros
Studios ........................... 2  E5

### ⌂ SHOP
8 Ball ................................ 3  D3
It's a Wrap ...................... 4  D3

Universal City
Walk ................................ 5  D6

### ⑪ EAT
Bob's Big Boy.................. 6  D4
Ca' del Sole .................... 7  C5
Minibar............................ 8  D6
Poquito Mas .................... 9  C6

### ⅄ DRINK
Firefly ........................... 10  A5

Please see over for map

# ◑ SEE

## ◎ UNIVERSAL STUDIOS

☎ 1-800-864-8377; www.universal
studioshollywood.com; 100 Universal
City Plaza, Universal City; admission
1-day pass over/under 48in tall $61/51,
front-of-the-line pass $109, Hollywood
City Pass, under 3yr free; ⏱ 10am-6pm
Mon-Fri, 9am-6pm Sat & Sun, extended
seasonally; Ⓜ Red Line to Universal City,
then free shuttle bus; Ⓟ ⓧ
The magic of movie-making gets
its due at ever-popular Universal,
where thrill rides, live performances, interactive shows and back-lot
tram tours perpetually draw the
masses. The *Revenge of the Mummy*
indoor roller-coaster and *Jurassic
Park* water ride lead the thrills while
several new theme-park and tour
attractions – *Shrek* in 4-D, the *War
of the Worlds* crash site and Wisteria
Lane from *Desperate Housewives*
(shooting dependent) – keep things
fresh. That said, some grumble that
too many attractions are dated. And
they may have a point – *Terminator
2: 3D*, *Water World* and *Backdraft*
aren't exactly new movies. With
cost, crowds and time factored in, it
can make one wonder if the whole
experience is worth it. But ending
the day with a tram tour should tip
the scales in favor of a yes. Cartoonish Whoville, a still-spooky Bates
motel and a tram-hungry shark still

*Water World* **warfare at Universal Studios**

reveal movie-making magic at its best. Parking costs $10.

### ⊙ WARNER BROS STUDIO VIP TOUR

☎ 818-972-8687; www.wbstudiotour
.com; 3400 Riverside Dr, Burbank;
2¼hr tour $45, under 8yr not admitted;
⏱ 8:30am-4pm; ⊞ MTA 96, 163; Ⓟ
After a 15-minute clip-filled short of WB's movie and TV highlights – from 'Stella!' to 'How you doin'? – VIPs board a 12-person open tram for a two-hour tour around the studio's 110-acre lot where secrets of Hollywood are revealed – forced perspective, fancy facades and fake bricks – or as one guide jauntily summed up, 'It's all lies and deceit.' Parking is through Gate 6 and costs $5. See also p10.

---

#### BE THE LAUGH TRACK

Half the fun of visiting Hollywood is hoping you might see a star, so up the odds with a visit to the set of a primetime sitcom. One-camera shows like *Two and a Half Men*, *The New Adventures of Old Christine* and *The King of Queens* are shot before a live audience. That's you. To nab tickets, check the website for Audiences Unlimited at www.tvtickets.com; to see what's taping, call ☎ 818-753-3470, or stop by the booth at Universal Studios (p137). For information on tickets for *The Tonight Show with Jay Leno* at NBC Studios, call ☎ 818-840-3537.

---

# 🛍 SHOP

### 🏷 8 BALL *Gifts*

☎ 818-845-1155; www.8ballwebstore
.com; 3806 W Magnolia Blvd; ⏱ 11am-
7pm Mon-Fri, 11am-6pm Sat, noon-5pm
Sun; ⊞ MTA 183
It's Vegas-kitsch with *Swingers* style at cosy 8 Ball, where leopard-print bowling shirts lounge beside tiki torches, Twinkie cookbooks and Betty Page heels. Frank and Elvis books flirt from shelves up front.

### 🏷 IT'S A WRAP *Clothing*

☎ 818-567-7366; www.itsawrap
hollywood.com; 3315 W Magnolia Blvd;
⏱ 11am-8pm Mon-Fri, to 6pm Sat &
Sun; ⊞ MTA 183
Dress just like your favorite movie stars – maybe in their actual clothes! This packed-to-the-rafters store sells clothing worn by cast members from TV and film. Persistence pays – from J Crew and Laura Ashley to Bebe and Juicy, the racks hold treasures galore. There's also a branch in **West LA** (☎ 310-246-9727; 1164 S Robertson Blvd).

### 🏷 UNIVERSAL CITY WALK *Outdoor Mall*

☎ 818-6220-4455; www.citywalk
hollywood.com; 1000 Universal City Dr;
⏱ 11am-9pm Sun-Thu, 11am-11pm Fri
& Sat; Ⓜ Universal City; Ⓟ ♿ ♗

High-end hand-me-downs at It's a Wrap

With flashing video screens, oversized facades and garish color combinations, City Walk hovers beside Universal Studios like a reject from the *Blade Runner*-meets-*Willy Wonka* school of architecture. Opened in 1993 as a shopping adjunct to the theme park, this outdoor mall evolved into a local's hangout that can feel like a middle school mecca on weekends. Its 65 shops, restaurants and entertainment venues offer a mix of mid- and low-brow attractions, with low leading by a nose. Beyond the knick-knack stores and chains, the new **Dodgers Clubhouse** ( ☎ 818-761-5677) stands out with its Dodgers-related clothing and accessories – including bats broken during games. The courtyard balcony at **Karl Strauss Brewery** (www.karlstrauss .com) is primo for people-watching while sipping a *hefeweizen*.

# 🍴 EAT

## 🍴 BOB'S BIG BOY *American* $
☎ 818-843-9334; www.bigboy.com;
4211 Riverside Dr; 🕑 24hr; 🚍 MTA 96,
152; 🚻 🛗

The red-checkered, pompadoured
kid still woos hamburger-craving
hordes at America's oldest remaining Big Boy's – his fiberglass form
a refreshing reminder that some
people in LA still eat. Inside, grab a
burnt-orange booth for a double-
decker combo, or, on weekend
nights, enjoy carhop service in
back.

## 🍴 CA' DEL SOLE *Italian* $$-$$$
☎ 818-985-4669; 4100 Cahuenga Blvd,
Toluca Lake; 🕑 11:30am-3pm Mon-Fri,
5-10:30pm Mon-Thu, 5-11pm Fri, 5:30-
11:30pm Sat, 11am-9pm Sun; 🚍 MTA 96

Sitting beside the fireplace within
the Mediterranean walls of Ca' del
Sole, it's easy to feel like one of
the Hollywood powerbrokers who
frequent the place. Efficient, low-
key service at this industry haven,
bordering NBC/Universal's busy
Gate 3, keeps dealmakers happy
while talking numbers over fresh
insalata di mare and pumpkin-
stuffed *mezzelune*.

Service with a smile at Bob's Big Boy

### 🍴 MINIBAR *Tapas* $$-$$$

☎ 323-882-6965; www.minibarlounge
.com; 3413 W Cahuenga Blvd; ⏱ 5:30-
10:30pm Mon-Thu & Sun, 5:30pm-1am Fri
& Sat; 🚌 156; Ⓥ

The stylishly stressed seek the
warm tones and tasty tapas of
Minibar after a hard day in the
studio mines – under somewhat
disconcerting portraits of wide-
eyed waifs. The menu, divided into
This, That & The Other, offers an
eclectic selection of delish small
plate specialties. The gouda-
stuffed yucca bread is a must. To
find it, look for the Valet of the
Dolls stand between Universal
Studios Blvd and Barham Blvd.

### 🍴 POQUITO MAS *Mexican* $

☎ 818-760-8226; www.poquitomas
.com; 3701 Cahuenga Blvd, Studio City;
⏱ 10am-midnight; Ⓜ Universal City;
Ⓥ ♿

Poquito Mas has fueled under-the-
gun TV writing staff since 1984 –
just ask the assistants who pick
up the massive orders. This local
fast-food chain serves up classic
Baja-style Mexican – fresh ingredients prepared with a light touch
(no lard). It's the hit-the-spot steak
burritos that best help writers
finesse that 3rd-act turn. Also in
**West Hollywood** (Map p63, C1; ☎ 310-652-
7008; 8555 Sunset Blvd).

# 🍸 DRINK

### 🍸 FIREFLY *Lounge*

☎ 818-762-1833; 11720 Ventura Blvd,
Studio City; ⏱ 6pm-2am Mon-Sat;
🚌 MTA 150, 240, 750

Firefly has the sexiest library this
side of an Anne Rice novel –
bordello-red lighting, low-slung
couches, flickering candles, all
surrounded by shelves of somber-
looking tomes. Not that anyone's
opened one. This upwardly mobile
crowd is too busy reading each
other. Don't waste time looking
for a sign – it's the ivy-covered
building with the valet stand.

### 🍸 SENOR FRED *Mexican Cantina*

☎ 818-789-3200; www.senorfred
.com; 13730 Ventura Blvd, Sherman
Oaks; ⏱ 11:30am-midnight Sun-Thu,
11:30am-2am Fri & Sat; 🚌 145, 240, 750

Fantastic happy-hour specials – $5
margaritas and sangrias – draw
Hollywood's up-and-comers to
this studio-central hangout. Sleek
but comfy lounges and Laker-
friendly TVs keep 'em loose, and
chatty, for hours.

# >PASADENA

Pasadena reigns from her lofty perch in the San Gabriel foothills like a beautiful Rose Bowl queen, collecting kudos that are, well, totally deserved. Wealthy Midwesterners were the first to succumb to her charms, coming west in the late 1880s for warmer weather and healthier climes. Fine Craftsmen homes like the Gamble House soon followed, their architectural style inspired by the gorgeous natural environs.

Pasadena's independent spirit and environmental-mindedness are evident today – from the popular Gold Line metro efficiently connecting citizens with downtown LA to pedestrian-friendly Old Town where shops, restaurants and conversations are footsteps away. The Tournament of Roses parade (p26), now in its 119th year, is so beloved that people camp out just to claim a sidewalk spot. Cultural assets abound, ranging from impressionist masterpieces at the Norton Simon to porcelain teacups at the Pacific Asia Museum to the Desert Garden at the Huntington. Pasadena's earned her tiara, and she's wearing it well.

## PASADENA

### ◉ SEE

### 🛍 SHOP

### 🍴 EAT

Please see over for map

Exquisite detail makes Gamble House a work of art

# SEE

## GAMBLE HOUSE

☎ 626-793-3334; www.gamblehouse
.org; 4 Westmoreland Pl; admission
adult/senior & student/under 12yr $10/7/
free; ⏱ noon-3pm Thu-Sun for guided
tours only; 🚌 MTA 267; 🅿

It's the exquisite attention to
detail that impresses most at
Gamble House, a masterpiece of
the Arts and Crafts style designed
by brothers Charles and Henry
Greene for Proctor & Gamble heir
David Gamble in the early 1900s.
The whole home is a work of
art, its foundation, furniture and
fixtures all united by a common
design and theme inspired by its
southern California environs. Note

sleeping porches, rounded corners
and subtle appearances of the
Gamble family crest's rose-and-
crane pattern.

## HUNTINGTON LIBRARY,
ART COLLECTIONS &
BOTANICAL GARDENS

☎ 626-405-2100; www.huntington
.org; 1151 Oxford Rd; adult/senior/stu-
dent/5-11yr/under 5yr $15/12/10/6/free;
⏱ 10:30am-4:30pm Tue-Sun Jun-Aug,
noon-4:30pm Tue-Fri, 10:30am-4:30pm
Sat & Sun Sep-May; 🚌 MTA 177; 🅿 ♿

Unwind in the zenlike tranquility
of the Japanese Garden? Study the
jaunty pose of Thomas Gains-
borough's *Blue Boy*? Linger over
the well-thumbed pages of the

NEIGHBORHOODS

PASADENA

See, smell and savor serenity at Huntington's Japanese Garden (p145)

Gutenberg Bible, the world's first printed book? It's hard to know where to start at this inspirational collection of botanical gardens, art and literature amassed by railroad magnate Henry E Huntington and displayed on his former estate. Inspirational beauty deserves exquisite cuisine, so ponder your options over the beloved English tea and sandwich service at the **Rose Garden Room** ( ☎ 626-683-8131; ⏲ noon-3:30pm Tue-Fri, 10:45am-3:30pm Sat & Sun) just past the quote-filled flora of the Shakespeare Garden (reservations recommended).

### ◎ NORTON SIMON MUSEUM
☎ 626-449-6840; www.nortonsimon .org; 411 W Colorado Blvd; adult/ senior/student & under 18yr $10/4/free; ⏲ noon-6pm Wed, Thu & Sat-Mon, to 9pm Fri; Ⓜ Memorial Park; Ⓟ ♿ ⚥

Norton Simon's passion for the arts shines through at this accessible museum – see Rodin's *The Thinker* luring visitors out front – thought by many to be the best collection of fine art in LA. The permanent exhibits, spanning the 14th century to the 20th and including Southeast Asian sculpture, fill six galleries over two floors.

### ◎ PACIFIC ASIA MUSEUM
☎ 626-449-2742; www.pacificasia museum.org; 46 N Los Robles Ave; adult/senior & student $7/5, 4th Fri of month free; ⏲ 10am-6pm Wed-Sun; Ⓜ Memorial Park

The Pacific Museum may be small, but with more than 14,000 works of Asian and Pacific Island art in its collection, the quality and range of the exhibits is almost unrivaled. The nine galleries, linked around a courtyard, include informative, accessible displays on Chinese, Tibetan, Southeast Asian and Japanese arts. The two-room Chinese Ceramics exhibit is fascinating.

# 🛍 SHOP

Angelenos wanting a friendly, small-town vibe, without spending more than 45 minutes to get there, often head to Pasadena's charming Old Town, a restored historic district jammed with 22 blocks of shops and restaurants.

## 📷 DISTANT LANDS TRAVEL BOOKSTORE & OUTFITTERS
*Travel*
☎ 626-449-3220; www.distantlands .com; 56 S Raymond Ave; 🕙 11am-6pm Sun & Mon, 10:30am-7pm Tue-Thu, 10:30am-9pm Fri & Sat, extended hours Apr-Sep; Ⓜ Memorial Park
Travel junkies jonesin' for a jaunt can feed their fix at Distant Lands. With comfy couches, loads of travel wear, knowledgeable staff and shelves stacked with guides from Alaska to Zimbabwe, vagabonds will stay all day or flee in minutes, guidebook and map firmly in hand.

## 📷 LUSH *Bath & Cosmetics*
☎ 626-792-0901; www.lush.com; 24 E Colorado Blvd; 🕙 11am-8pm Mon-Thu, to 9pm Fri & Sat, to 7pm Sun; Ⓜ Memorial Park

Scrubbing bubbles never looked so good. In fact, the homemade bath bombs loading the bins at this soap-scented store look so fresh, fruity and fancy that you're almost tempted to take a bite. But no worries here, the fun-loving staff are happy to explain the proper path for primo sudsy pampering.

## 📷 VROMAN'S BOOKSTORE
*Books*
☎ 626-449-5320; www.vromans bookstore.com; 695 E Colorado Blvd; 🕙 9am-9pm Mon-Thu, 9am-10pm Fri & Sat, 10am-8pm Sun; 🚍 MTA 686; 🚶
Loiterers and laptops are welcome at friendly Vroman's, SoCal's oldest and largest independent bookstore. Working hard to keep customers happy, Vroman's has wi-fi, weekly story times, a MySpace page, a blog, a coffee shop and regular author signings. Inveterate bookhounds and page-flippers love the combined 85,000-book inventory.

# 🍴 EAT

## 🍴 ALL INDIA CAFÉ *Indian* $-$$
☎ 626-440-0309; www.allindiacafe .com; 39 S Fair Oaks Ave; 🕙 11:30am-10pm Sun-Thu, to 11pm Fri & Sat; Ⓜ Memorial Park
To escape the Old Town hustle-and-bustle, look no further than this inviting café. While lazy ceiling fans, exposed brick walls and

embroidered tapestries create the illusion of faraway travels, it's chef Santokh Singh's tenderly flavored regional specialties – chicken tikka masala, shrimp curry vindaloo, garlic nan – that make the journey complete.

## 🍴 BAR CELONA Spanish $$-$$$
☎ 626-405-1000; www.barcelona pasadena.com; 46 E Colorado Blvd; 🕑 11am-1:30am; Ⓜ Memorial Park; Ⓥ

Fine diners savor seafood paellas and wine-braised steaks in Bar Celona's candlelit dining room while sangria-sipping hipsters linger in the late-night lounge. Between the two scenes, chefs impress with exotic small-plate specials at the happenin' tapas bar.

## 🍴 EUROPANE Bakery $
☎ 626-577-1828; 950 E Colorado Blvd; 🕑 7am-5:30pm Mon-Sat, to 2pm Sun; 🚍 MTA Memorial Park; Ⓥ 👶

With its concrete floors, small wooden tables and jumbled baskets of unmarked pastries, Europane doesn't exactly ooze warmth. But buttery bearclaws, fluffy croissants and smooth cups of coffee make up for any lack of coffeehouse coziness. Arrive early for croissants; they sell out.

## 🍴 MIJARES MEXICAN RESTAURANT Mexican $-$$
☎ 626-792-2763; www.mijares restaurant.com; 145 Palmetto Dr; 🕑 11am-9pm Mon-Thu, 1am-10pm Fri & Sat, 9:30am-10pm Sun; 🚍 MTA; Ⓟ 👶

Pasadeneans have flocked to the tapestry-lined walls of sprawling Mijares for almost 90 years. Although the focus is more on fun than fine cuisine, addictive chips and salsa, traditional combo platters and powerful margaritas keep the patios filled with families, friendsters and a business team or two. Try the yummy avocado- and chip-filled tortilla soup.

## 🍴 SALADANG SONG Thai $$
☎ 626-793-5200; 383 S Fair Oaks Ave; 🕑 7am-9:45pm Sun-Thu, to 10pm Fri & Sat; Ⓜ 686, 687

Inside the soaring glass walls of Saladang Song, it's the details that first impress – a bright flower on every table, efficient service, artfully presented food. But the first bite of one of their beloved Thai specialties brings it all home. Song serves light, fusion-friendly Thai – sassy salads, spicy wraps and savory soups – while sister restaurant Saladang next door offers a more traditional Thai menu.

# >ORANGE COUNTY

Classic Googie architecture at Laguna Beach (p157)

# ORANGE COUNTY

## DISNEYLAND & DISNEY'S CALIFORNIA ADVENTURE

Mickey is one lucky mouse. Created by animator Walt Disney in 1928, this irrepressible rodent caught a ride on a multimedia juggernaut – film, TV, publishing, music, merchandising and theme parks – that's rocketed him into a global stratosphere of recognition, wealth and influence. Not to mention he lives in the Happiest Place on Earth, a slice of 'imagineered' hyperreality where the streets are always clean, the park employees – called cast members – are always upbeat, and there's a parade every day of the year. It would be easy to hate the guy, but since opening his home to guests in 1955, he's been a pretty thoughtful host to millions and millions of visitors.

Entering the Magic Kingdom, you'll pass under an archway reading 'Here you leave today and enter the world of yesterday, tomorrow, and fantasy,' an apt but slightly skewed welcome that's a bit indicative of the upbeat, slightly skewed 'reality' of the park itself.

Guests funnel onto **Main Street, USA**, an idyllic representation of an early-1900s small town complete with barbershop quartet, penny arcades, ice-cream shoppes and a steam train. Modeled after Disney's boyhood home in Marcilene, Missouri, the streets look longer and taller than they really are due to forced perspective, a trick used on Hollywood sets when buildings are constructed at a decreasing scale to create an illusion of height or depth.

---

### INFORMATION

**Location** 1313 Harbor Blvd, Anaheim (25 miles southeast of downtown LA on I-5, exit Disneyland Dr)

**Getting there** 🚌 MTA 460 from downtown LA (1½ hours)

**Contact** ☎ 714-781-4565, live assistance ☎ 714-781-7290, www.disneyland.com, www.disneytravel.com

**Costs** One-day single park ticket adult/three to nine years/under three years $63/53/free, dual park passes $83/73/free, SoCal CityPass (boxed text, p43)

**Opening hours** Disneyland 🕙 9am-8pm/10pm, extended summer hours 8am to midnight; DCA 🕙 10am to 6pm, extended summer hours 8am to 10pm

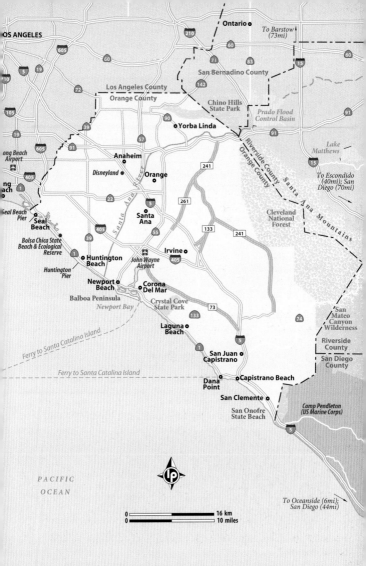

On Main Street there's a 20-minute parade every evening. Check with Information for start times then situate early for a top sidewalk spot. There are fireworks nightly in summer, around 9:30pm.

Main Street ends at **Central Plaza**, where the Partners statue of Walt and Mickey lords over its domain. This is the park's hub, with five spokes extending to the eight different 'lands.' Take a moment to appreciate the pink confection in front of you, **Sleeping Beauty's Castle**, Disney's most recognizable icon after you-know-who.

To the right of the plaza is **Tomorrowland**, a vision of what imagineers thought the future might look like back in the 1950s – monorails, rockets and Googie-like architecture, it seems. Today, most of the attractions have been updated and the biggest thrills come from *Star Wars*–inspired Star Tours with its buffeting StarSpeeder rocketing through a big-screen, slightly nauseating deep space. Space Mountain, with its tight turns, screaming drops and blaring music, remains one of the park's most adrenaline-filled attractions. Classic stories and characters dwell in **Fantasyland**, where the canal ride through multilingual versions of 'It's a Small World' still charms the kiddies. For a surprisingly irreverent little trip, hop aboard Mr Toad's Wild Ride, inspired by *The Wind in the Willows*, for a loopy jaunt through Mr Toad's mansion, underground London, Winky's Pub and, sadly, the courthouse. The Big Thunder Mountain Railroad rollercoaster awaits in **Frontierland**, where pioneers, miners and Tom Sawyer live on. **New Orleans Square** houses the spooky, but not too scary, Haunted Mansion as well as the ever-popular 16-minute Pirates of the Caribbean boat-ride. Indiana Jones beckons from **Adventureland** with a lurching drive on an oversized jeep through an archaeologist's worst nightmare.

Across the entry plaza is the resort's newest addition, Disney's California Adventure (DCA), which opened in 2001. A 50ft sun greets visitors in Sunshine Plaza, where God, I mean Michael Eisner, tells us on a plaque

---

**TOP FIVE DISNEYLAND DON'T-MISS ATTRACTIONS**
> Space Mountain (Tomorrowland)
> Indiana Jones (Adventureland)
> Mr Toad's Wild Ride (Fantasyland)
> Pirates of the Caribbean (New Orleans Square)
> Haunted Mansion (New Orleans Square)

**TOP FIVE DCA DON'T-MISS ATTRACTIONS**
> California Screamin' (Paradise Pier)
> Soarin' Over California (Golden State)
> Tower of Terror (Hollywood Pictures Backlot)
> Grizzly River Run (Golden State)
> Tough to be a Bug (A Bug's Land)

## TOP DISNEYLAND TIPS

> At a minimum, plan on at least one day for each park. Saturday is busiest year-round, with Monday and Friday next busiest in summer. The week before Christmas, with the holiday decorations, is also crowded. To avoid jams, try spring, fall or right after Labor Day. February is ideal.

> Study a map before pushing through the turnstiles. Strategy is the key to happiness.

> Stop at free Fastpass kiosks with your ticket, and you'll be assigned an hour-long frame within which to enjoy an attraction. With it, you can cut to the front of the line.

> Many rides have minimum age and height requirements; avoid tantrums, and prep the kids.

> Your bags will be searched at the turnstiles. Food and drink, but not bombs, are okay. Pocket knives can't be brought into the park but can be checked with security and picked up on the way back out.

that the park celebrates the richness and diversity of California, its land, its people and 'the dreams that it continues to inspire.' The state's biggest factory of dreams is Tinsel Town, repped here in the **Hollywood Pictures Backlot**. Crowds stream to the 183ft-tall Twilight Zone Tower of Terror where views of the San Gabriel mountains – from a plummeting elevator – are amazing, if slightly brief. In **Golden State**, the simulated hang-gliders of Soarin' Over California swoop over thrilling IMAX images of California's scenic highlights. Get wet on the Grizzly River Run or sample Napa wine on the terrace at **Golden Vine Winery**. From there, enjoy perfect views of **Paradise Pier**, a seaside resort of yesteryear where the hurtling California Screamin' coaster and a 150ft Ferris wheel await. Rollercoaster newbies may prefer the Mulholland Madness minicoaster.

Just outside the parks you'll find Downtown Disney, a quarter-mile-long pedestrian mall crowded with shops, restaurants, entertainment venues and tourists. The massive World of Disney store offers every Disney product under the sun – perhaps the most memorable is a black hoodie perfect for park-weary curmudgeons that's labeled simply: 'Grouchy'.

On site, the 990 rooms of the **Disneyland Hotel** ( ☎ 714-778-6600; 1150 Magic Way) offer family-friendly lodging in sleek, slightly retro towers. Although the hotel is only a short walk from Disneyland, use the adjacent monorail for a quick, fun ride right into the park. The newest Disney lodging is the stunning Arts & Crafts–style **Grand Californian Hotel** ( ☎ 714-635-2300; 1600 S Disneyland Dr), its massive timber beams and cavernous lobby reminiscent of the grand lodges of our national parks. In fact, relaxing on the lobby's massive

ORANGE COUNTY

couches while listening to a piano player may cause you to feel as if you're cheating on Yosemite's rustic Ahwahnee Hotel or Yellowstone's towering Old Faithful Inn – and enjoying the illicit affair just a little too much.

# ORANGE COUNTY BEACHES

If you're curious about the reality *behind* the reality of Bravo's *The Real Housewives of Orange County* and MTV's *Laguna Beach*, then a trip to the OC's gorgeous beach communities is a must. The county's northern-most coastal hideaways are Seal Beach and Huntington Beach, the latter boasting the 'Surf City, USA' moniker as well as the **International Surfing Museum** ( ☎ 714-960-3483; www.surfingmuseum.org; 411 Olive Ave) and though both communities are scenic and well-to-do, they're just a bit too sincere to be the focus of unscripted drama.

Nope, the glitz starts at **Newport Beach**, where the Botox-and-Beamers philosophy is evident at every turn. From big-box mansions dotting the coast to sparkling yachts riding the swell, life is good and everyone needs to know. The one place that remains somewhat real is the beach, best seen from 6-mile-long **Balboa Peninsula** in the middle of Newport's natural harbor. For a striking architectural specimen, stroll past the 1926 **Lovell House** (1242 W Ocean Front), designed by seminal modernist architect Rudolf Schindler. Restaurants and bars cluster near the two piers – Newport Pier to the west and Balboa Pier to the southeast – or skip all that and get your kicks on the Ferris wheel at the **Balboa Fun Zone** ( ☎ 949-673-0408; www .thebalboafunzone.com; 603 E Bay Ave; ☼ 11am-7pm Sun-Thu, to 9pm Fri, to 10pm Sat), here since 1936. A five-minute **ferry ride** (car & drive $1.50, adult/5-11yr/under 5yr $0.60/0.30/free; ☼ 6:30am-midnight Mon-Thu, to 2am Fri & Sat) drops visitors on cottage- and shop-filled **Balboa Island**. For sun-dappled fun, stroll the 1½-mile promenade encircling the island. Sunsets are amazing.

Just south of Balboa Peninsula is **Corona Del Mar**, a ritzy bedroom community on the privileged eastern flanks of the Newport Channel with plenty of upscale stores and restaurants. **Corona del Mar State Beach** ( ☎ 949-644-3151; ☼ 5am-10pm) lies at the foot of the cliffs. Locals enjoy impromptu,

---

## DISTANCES FROM DOWNTOWN LA
> Huntington Beach – 37 miles
> Newport Beach – 44 miles
> Laguna Beach – 51 miles

Dudes and dunes at Laguna Beach

not quite legal, cocktail parties at **Lookout Point**, perched above the beach. Corona del Mar's prize attraction is the **Sherman Library & Gardens** ( ☎ 949-673-2261; www.slgardens.org; 2647 E Pacific Coast Hwy; adult/12-16yr $3/1, Mon free; ☼ gardens 10:30am-4pm, library 9am-4:30pm Tue-Thu), where a variety of lush gardens awaits those needing a quick dose of floral therapy.

Secluded beaches, low cliffs and glassy waves await just a few miles south in the long-time artist enclave, **Laguna Beach**. This coastal paradise was jostled in the summer of 2005 after mudslides, instigated by wet winter weather, destroyed or severely damaged about two dozen cliff-side homes. While the town and the *Laguna Beach* cast soldier on, you're best to visit sooner rather than later – there are hints that this open-minded, indie-spirited town, known for its gay-friendly vibe, is on the tipping point of cookie-cutter as many older businesses shut their doors to make room for the trendy. For now, check out the shops, restaurants and galleries clustered in the Village along Broadway, Ocean and Forest. The permanent collection in the breezy **Laguna Art Museum** ( ☎ 949-494-8971; www.lagunaartmuseum.org; 307 Cliff Dr; adult/senior, student, active duty military & dependents/under 13yr $10/8/free; ☼ 11am-5pm) is heavy on California landscapes and vintage photographs, while rotating exhibits usually spotlight California artists. As for Laguna's beaches, **Main Beach** provides volleyball and basketball courts and is the best for swimming. Savor sweeping views of craggy coves and deep-blue sea from bluff-top **Heisler Park**.

Welcome to La La Land, the city of reinvention where you can be anyone you want to be – if only for the weekend. That dress you'd never wear at home? The faux-hawk you're daring to sport? Now's the time. Just use the keys below to unlock doors to the best LA has to offer.

Famous faces in the Hollywood Museum (p42)

# ACCOMMODATIONS

When choosing overnight digs in Los Angeles, the primo decision is location. Staying at a posh Santa Monica beach hotel is probably not the best choice if you're catching a performance at Walt Disney Concert Hall downtown or visiting Universal Studios in Burbank. It can be done, but your happiness quotient will rise or fall depending how long you're sitting in your car. That said, most neighborhoods have hotels in just about every price range, though expect to pay between $100 and $200 per night for a midrange room.

Sun, sand and surf on the agenda? For upscale sparkle, try Santa Monica's **Shutters on the Beach** (www.shuttersonthebeach.com) or Manhattan Beach's spanking-new **Shade** (www.shadehotel.com). If swanky's not a concern, low-key **Sea Shore Motel** (www.seashoremotel.com) on Santa Monica's Main St is keen while the bright **Hermosa Hotel** (www.hotelhermosa.com) on the Pacific Coast Hwy suits South Bay sun-worshippers.

In Beverly Hills, discretion and charm have lured guests to the pink, very posh **Beverly Hills Hotel** (www.thebeverlyhillshotel.com) since 1912. And yes, Marilyn Monroe slept here. In fact, she seems to have slept everywhere, including the **Avalon Hotel** (www.avalonbeverlyhills.com), a fashion-crowd fave seen in *Dream Girls*. Cozy **Maison 140** (www.maison140.com), once a boarding house run by Lillian Gish, is nearby. In Culver City, the quirky, few-frills **Culver Hotel** (www.culverhotel.com) offers history – the munchkins stayed here while filming *The Wizard of Oz* – as well as proximity to theaters and restaurants.

Heading north to Sunset Strip, famed celeb hideaway **Chateau Marmont** (www.chateaumarmont.com) lurks like a Transylvanian castle but rockers, starlets

Haystack is Lonely Planet's online accommodations booking service. Over 60 properties are featured for Los Angeles – each personally inspected, thoroughly reviewed and happily recommended by a Lonely Planet author. From hostels to high-end hotels, we've hunted out the places that will bring you unique and special experiences. Read independent reviews by authors and other travelers, and get practical information including amenities, maps and photos. Then reserve your room simply and securely via Haystack – our online booking service. It's all at www.lonelyplanet.com/accommodation.

and Matthew McConaughey seem to like it that way. One of the Strip's best deals is Best Western's centrally located **Sunset Plaza** (www.sunsetplazahotel.com).

Moving east, the **Renaissance Hollywood** (www.renaissancehollywood.com), behind the Hollywood & Highland complex, offers loads of amenities. Ask for a view of the Hollywood sign. Nearby, the historic, revamped **Hollywood Roosevelt** (www.hollywoodroosevelt.com) curries favor with Hollywood scenesters despite its uncanny resemblance to the Tower of Terror at Disney's California Adventure.

Just south, the flirty, faux-country charms of the **Farmers Daughter** (www.farmersdaughterhotel.com) lure a mixed-interest crew – museum hoppers, power shoppers and potential game-show contestants at nearby CBS studios. For reasonably priced retro flair, try the **Beverly Laurel Motor Hotel** ( ☎ 323-651-2441). In Burbank, Beverly Garland's **Holiday Inn** (www.beverlygarland.com) is always reliable.

Downtown, Moroccan-themed **Hotel Figueroa** (www.figueroahotel.com) draws a young crowd as well as conventioneers. The mod downtown **Standard** (www.standardhotel.com), with its rooftop bar and hipper-than-thou decor, is a rowdier option.

## INTERNET RESOURCES

In addition to www.lonelyplanet.com/accommodation, check www.losangeles.com for hotel 'hot rates.' Online agencies such as www.orbitz.com, www.expedia.com, www.travelocity.com and www.hotel.com offer bargains, but always compare their deals with the rates on the hotel's own website. Peruse www.kayak.com and www.sidestep.com for comprehensive comparisons of the best rates offered by the online agencies – a data crush that can quicken your search or delay it, depending on your handling of massive amounts of information.

### MOST HISTORIC HOTELS

> Beverly Hills Hotel (www.thebeverlyhillshotel.com)
> Chateau Marmont (www.chateaumarmont.com)
> Culver Hotel (www.culverhotel.com)
> Hollywood Roosevelt (www.hollywoodroosevelt.com)
> Avalon (www.avalonbeverlyhills.com)

### BEST ON A BUDGET

> Beverly Laurel Motor Hotel ( ☎ 323-651-2441)
> Best Western Sunset Plaza (www.sunsetplazahotel.com)
> Sea Shore Motel (www.seashoremotel.com)
> Culver Hotel (www.culverhotel.com)
> Hotel Hermosa (www.hotelhermosa.com)

# ARCHITECTURE

When discussing LA's most influential architects it's tempting to mention the names Frank Lloyd Wright, Frank Gehry and Richard Meier and call it a day. But that would be unfair to the two other guys. It would also be ignoring the relatively short but fascinating history of LA's iconic buildings and architectural styles that have incorporated the city's cultural zeitgeist as well as its stunning landscapes.

At the turn of the 19th century, new residents were arriving en masse from the Midwest, seeking better weather and healthier climes. Pasadena was the neighborhood of choice among the wealthiest, and Arts and Crafts homes, as popularized by brothers Charles and Henry Greene, were the style of choice. With its fine wood craftsmanship, Asian-inspired design and flowing open-air style, the Gamble House (p145) is the most stunning example of Greene and Greene design – a style soon emulated in bungalows all the way to West Hollywood. Frank Lloyd Wright was designing homes in the Romanza style a few years later – for every indoor space there's an outdoor space – and this flowing design is best exhibited in the Hollyhock House (p55) he constructed for heiress Aline Barnsdale.

In the 1920s LA wanted to flex its muscle on the national scene and needed the appropriate downtown landmarks to inspire respect. The stunning Richard J Riordan Central Library (see the boxed text, p129) was finished in 1926, complete with 64ft-high dome, breathtaking murals and a 9ft chandelier. The 32-story City Hall, an exception to the city's earthquake-conscious height limit, was completed two years later. Hollywood's grand, often ornate, movie palaces were also opening their doors in what was perhaps one of the most exciting decades for this burgeoning city.

A few of LA's quirkier buildings were constructed in the decades to come. The most iconic include the 1950s Googie coffeehouses with their neon, space-age style as well as LAX's spindly, futuristic white Theme Building (where the bar with lava-lamp cool, Encounters, has temporarily closed due to structural concerns). West Hollywood's gargantuan Pacific Design Center (p64) – dubbed The Blue Whale – has garnered stares since 1975. According to the *Los Angeles Times*, its monochromatic blue and green buildings will soon be joined by a red, fin-shaped companion.

Some of the landscape's most exciting landmarks have arrived in the last two decades. Richard Meier's hilltop Getty Center (p83), a marvel of sweeping stone, terraces and gardens, opened in 1996, wowing Westsiders from its lofty hilltop perch. Downtown, the Jose Rafael's Cathedral of Our Lady of the Angels (p125), completed in 2002, strikes a lofty, contemporary pose on Bunker Hill high above the I-101, hopefully inspiring drivers to consider the bigger picture. A few blocks away, the billowing, silver curves of Frank Gehry's 2003 Walt Disney Concert Hall (p129) have become downtown's most iconic architectural feature. In the next few years, the Grand Avenue project, with its stores, residents and restaurants, will bring even more changes to the Bunker Hill skyline.

One of the more interesting – or depressing – developments has been the proliferation of malls designed in an over-the-top style not befitting the surrounding landscape – from the cartoonish facades of Universal City Walk (p140) to the faux-Italian-village stylings of The Grove (p75). Despite shudders from traditionalists, however, these 'themed lifestyle centers' are actually drawing massive crowds and their central spaces are perpetually filled with people – many just relaxing and enjoying the scene. It can be argued that no matter how faux, fab or frightening the backdrop, there's something to be said for the cross-cultural community created daily in these outdoor malls – especially in a self-absorbed city typically known for drive-alone sprawl.

**BEST ARCHITECTURAL TOURS**
> Walt Disney Concert Hall (p129)
> Gamble House (p145)
> Hollyhock House (right; p55)

**MOST LIKELY TO LEAVE AN IMPRESSION**
> Walt Disney Concert Hall (p129)
> Pacific Design Center (p64)
> Richard J Riordan Central Library (boxed text; p129)
> Cathedral of Our Lady of the Angels (p125)
> Theme Building (LAX; p191)

# CELEBRITY SPOTTING

Let's just admit why you're here, shall we? You may say you're in LA to attend a convention, to take depositions, to sit through a seminar, but that's not the full story, is it? C'mon, you jumped at the chance, didn't you? There was that glimmer of possibility, that unspoken hope, that you might see…Laura Ingalls. Or Peter Brady. Heck, even Rob and Amber would be more interesting than those losers at the office.

And that's OK. Mankind's been worshipping celebrities since the first Neanderthal did that funny little number by the campfire. Even the Wiggles have groupies. Prophets, poets, professional actors – people are drawn to a famous face. Maybe it's the talent we love, or feeling connected to the world through one anointed person, or thinking we'll absorb a bit of the holy glow. Or maybe they're just hot. The University of Southern California published a study finding that actors and actresses tend to be more narcissistic than the rest of society. Uh, yeah, and too much cheese is fattening. That being said, it suggests that fan-love sates their needs as well as your own.

So how to fulfill two needs with one gawk? Driving past stars' homes is a start, but it's unlikely you'll see anyone. As for velvet-rope clubs, you probably won't get in and the doorman might hurt your feelings. And really, who needs that? So where to look for stars? In their natural habitat, of course.

Restaurants are primo, especially in Hollywood, West Hollywood and Mid-City. Those with patios and hidden nooks, even better. Coffee-wise, try stylish Urth Caffé (pictured left; p68) on Melrose Ave, where starlets, fashionistas and wannabes battle for the best patio perches. As for theaters, spotting celebs at the ArcLight (p48) is like shooting ducks from a blind; keep your eyes open and they'll eventually fly by. Shopping works too. Stores can't survive on Lindsay and Britney alone, so browse their faves on Robertson Blvd and Melrose Ave. Finally, hillside trails are favored for exercise. Who knows who's jogging past in that baseball cap.

Check out www.defamer.com or www.tmz.com for the latest sightings; they're usually right on. HBO's *Entourage* is good too. The *LA Times* Thursday Calendar section runs 'My Favorite Weekend,' where celebs spill their favorite haunts.

Once you've spotted one? See the boxed text, p80.

## BEST CELEBRITY-SPOTTING RESTAURANTS
> Koi (p66)
> M Café de Chaya (p79)
> AOC (p78)
> Campanile (p78)
> Toast Bakery Café (p80)

## BEST CINEMAS FOR STAR SIGHTINGS
> ArcLight Cinemas (p48)
> Pacific Theaters at The Grove (p75)

## POPULAR CELEB SHOPPING SPOTS
> Fred Segal (p65)
> Kitson (p65)
> Montana Ave (p94)
> The Grove (p75)

## CELEB SIGHTING ALMOST GUARANTEED
> Runyon Canyon (boxed text, p55)
> Koi (p66)
> Urth Caffé (p68)
> Chateau Marmont (p160)
> Warner Bros Studio Tour (p10)

# DRINKING

It's the old-school bars you'll remember most. Low on attitude, long on history. In fact, looking up from your bar-side perch within the dark confines of the Formosa Café (p68), you half expect Bogie to stroll in through the door and grab the seat next to you, as if the guy had never left. Same thing up the road at Musso & Frank Grill (p47) on Hollywood Blvd, where they've served no-frills martinis to moody writers – Fitzgerald, Chandler and Hammer – for the better part of a century.

At Dan Tana's (p66) tiny, elbow-to-elbow bar in West Hollywood, the low-key bartenders know how to make a drink while keeping the conversation cool, a seductive combo that's kept A-listers stopping by for years. Same thing at the Polo Lounge (p93), where moguls and movie stars of every generation still make the scene, not to mention deals, from dimly lit booths surrounding the bar. And you'll be treated like a star yourself – from the moment a smiling, pink-shirted valet takes your rental, it seems your close-up is seconds away. It is the Beverly Hills Hotel after all.

But don't worry, there are more places to get your drink on than a few retro bars. Trust me, you can't take three steps in this town without bumping into a Bluetoothed bouncer blocking an unmarked door. What's he guarding? Tented cabanas, flickering votives, sleek ottomans, exposed brick walls and martini-sipping scenesters clutching their Blackberries. It's the checklist for any LA lounge hoping to earn its street cred.

But no LA trip is complete without a sunset cocktail. For seaside views, grab a seat at the Bluewater Grill (p120), Hennessey's Tavern (p122), or the Lobster (p105). For a stellar citywide backdrop, savor the sunset from the rooftop bar at the Standard (p134). It will make your life just a little bit better.

### BEST MARGARITAS
> El Cholo (p103)
> El Coyote Mexican Café (p81)
> El Conquistador (p59)
> Mijares Mexican Restaurant (p150)
> Velvet Margarita (p48)

### BEST GASTROPUBS
> Bowery (p47)
> Father's Office (p106)
> Library Alehouse (p104)
> Village Idiot (p81)

### BEST PATIOS
> Cat & Fiddle (p47)
> Abbey (p67)
> Edendale Grill Mixville Bar (p60)
> On the Waterfront Cafe (p115)

### BEST DRINKS WITH A VIEW
> Standard Rooftop Bar (p134)
> Neptune's Net (boxed text, p104)
> Hennessey's Tavern (p122)
> Skybar (p68)
> Hump (p104)

**Top left** Hollywood old-timer Musso & Frank Grill **Above** Converted gothic monastery, Abbey (p67)

# FOOD

If you ask a native what they like most about LA, you'll probably hear, 'There's so much food to choose from!' From Ethiopian to Mexican to Vietnamese, if you're craving it, they're serving it somewhere within the city's 465 sq miles. Although the focus recently has held tight on tapas, spicy tuna and Kobe beef, at least we're past the gourmet pizza craze. Or not.

But first things first. When choosing a restaurant, don't let decor be the deciding factor. Yes, some of the best-designed LA restaurants offer exquisite cuisine – like Crustacean (p89), O-Bar (p67) and Koi (p66) – but some of the tastiest meals come from concrete-floor joints like Square One Dining (p59), Europane (p150), Roscoe's House of Chicken & Waffles (p45) and tiny Yuca's taco hut (p60), which sits on a concrete parking lot. As for strip-mall eateries and four-wheeled taco trucks, if you see a line, don't be a snob – join in.

Another trick is following the chef. Some of LA's best have been on a restaurant-opening binge, and that's where gourmands are heading. Celebs Wolfgang Puck and Joachim Splichal are always up to something, but smaller-scale owner-chefs have been opening exciting new restaurants too – aficionados of Suzanne Goin's popular Luques, housed in Harold Lloyd's cozy carriage house, followed her to AOC (p78) and Hungry Cat (p44). Nancy Silverton just opened hot, hot, hot Pizzeria Mozza (p80), her years at La Brea Bakery and Campanile (p78) putting this venture with Mario Batali in good stead.

So how to find great chefs in the first place? Visit www.cookslibrary .com or stop by Cook's Library (p77) on W 3rd St to see what local chefs are up to cookbook-wise, or just to talk food. As for foodie websites, the passionate debates on LA cuisine at www.chowhound.com can be informative as well as amusing.

Finally, not to be a scold, but glance at the Health Department rating that must be prominently posted at LA restaurants. As are preferred, of course, but occasional Bs can be forgiven – except when it comes to sushi. Anything below a B? Caveat emptor.

But overall, dining here is a grade A experience. Fish and chips, gumbo, slippery shrimp, pad thai, chicken vindaloo, fried chicken, cous cous salad – I could continue but it's time to eat!

### BEST BURGER
> Hungry Cat (p44)
> Bowery (p47)
> Father's Office (p106)
> Counter (p103)
> In-n-Out Burger (boxed text, p47)

### BEST NO-FRILLS DINING
> Sanamluang Café (p46)
> Yuca's (p60)
> Square One Dining (p59)
> Europane (p150)
> Skooby's (p46)

### BEST DESSERTS
> Sweet Lady Jane (p67)
> Three Square Bakery & Café (p114)
> Sprinkles Cupcakes (p92)
> O-Bar (p67)
> Boule (p65)

### BEST TAPAS
> Primitivo Wine Bistro (p114)
> AOC (p78)
> Minibar (p143)

**Top left** Fruit served the Mexican way on Olvera St **Above** Father's Office (p106), home to more than 30 beers on tap

SNAPSHOTS

# MUSEUMS

So many wonderful museums, so little time. So how best to tackle LA's finest? Location, location, location – determine your interests then consider your time frame. Many of LA's best demand a day-long visit, while others are perfect for a drop-by between shopping, dining and celeb-hunting. It's Destination vs Pop-in, and either choice has its charms.

One of the most popular destination museums is the Getty Center (p83). Because of its unique transportation system – an electric tram whisks guests up to the top of a hill – as well an extensive mix of art, gardens, views and cafés, expect a visit to take the better part of a day. Same with Pasadena's Huntington Gardens (p145). Unless you're staying in Pasadena, expect a 45-minute drive to get there. Once on the grounds, sprawling gardens, stunning exhibits and a charming café will inspire a strong desire to linger. Expect to spend the better part of the day at the museums in Exposition Park. The Natural History Museum (p129) is jam-packed with natural wonders, while the interactive displays at the neighboring California Science Center (p125) will keep you learning all afternoon. Same with the Los Angeles County Museum of Art (LACMA; p71) on Wilshire. Not only are there an astounding number of masterpieces on site, but next door the Page Museum at the La Brea Tar Pits (p71) provides a sticky review of LA's prehistoric treasures.

No time for all that? Plenty of smaller museums focus on one type of art, history or culture that can be immensely entertaining, not to mention more quickly enjoyed. Cubicle cowboys will fancy the Museum of the American West (p56) in Griffith Park, while porcelain junkies can get their fix at Pasadena's Pacific Asia Museum (p148). For an afternoon mind fracture there's downtown's bright Museum of Contemporary Art (MOCA; p128) where the exhibits are always engaging, if not always easy, or Culver City's sneaky Museum of Jurassic Technology (boxed text, p86) where exhibits aren't always what they seem.

And if all you want is a taste of Hollywood, LA's got that too. Try the kitschy charms of the Hollywood Museum (p42) or check out the extensive broadcast media collection at the Museum of Television & Radio (p87).

**MOST FUN MUSEUMS**
> Museum of the American West (p56)
> Natural History Museum (p129)
> Museum of Jurassic Technology (boxed text; p86)
> Hollywood Museum (p42)
> Huntington Library, Art Collections & Botanical Gardens (p145)

**CHARMINGLY SPECIFIC MUSEUMS**
> Petersen Automotive Museum (p74)
> Museum of Television & Radio (p87)
> Pacific Asia Museum (p148)
> Page Museum at the La Brea Tar Pits (p71)

**Top left** Suspended bicycle in the California Science Center (p125) **Above** Lobby of Hollywood Museum (p42)

SNAPSHOTS

# SHOPPING

Did Sir Edmund Hilary climb Everest without reconnaissance? Did John Glenn land on the moon without reading the rocket manual? Are you going to visit the world's premiere shopping mecca without a teensy bit of pre-trip prep? I didn't think so. Follow these guidelines and set your credit card free.

First, consider your preferred shopping experience then determine prime destinations based on your location and time frame. Because of sprawl and congestion, hopping between shopping spots isn't always easy.

If it's unique stores you're after, LA boasts boutique and indie-lined avenues all over town. In Santa Monica upscale women's wear beckons from tiny Montana Ave where babies and dogs are the accessory du jour. South of the I-10, Main St floats a beach-chic feel on oceanside breezes where flip-flop fashionistas and fashion-forward fellas dig the cool boutiques and low-key vibe. Everyone's talking about trendy Abbot Kinney Blvd (p17) just south in Venice where gift stores, bakeries and boho specialty stores cluster for a funky mix. All rise for venerable Melrose Ave – interior designers favor shops east of San Vicente near the Avenues of Arts & Design while the young and the skinny flock to the Crescent Heights intersection, anchored by star-friendly Fred Segal (p65). WeHo's Robertson Blvd claims the celebutante crown, where Kitson (p65) and Lisa Kline (p65) draw rehab-and-rebound royalty; Larchmont Ave, 3rd and La Cienega, and La Brea Ave should also get their avenue props.

Palazzo-style outdoor malls are also enormously popular. Although The Grove at 3rd and Fairfax Ave bursts with run-of-the-mill chain stores, its exuberant central fountain and faux-Italian charms prove irresistible to the masses. Sophisticated sibling Century City shines just west, where

Bloomingdales and Macy's anchor a swath of high-end chains. Santa Monica's Third St Promenade serves up three blocks of pedestrian-only shopping attracting an edgier, younger clientele.

In a class by itself is venerable Rodeo Dr, glistening like a perfectly cut diamond in the palm of Beverly Hills and attracting admirers from around the world to its high-end stores. At the opposite end of town, as well as the shopping spectrum, you'll find downtown's fashion district, a 90-block warren of stores and stalls awaiting the bargain hunter in us all.

For those about to shop, we envy you.

## BEST GIFT STORES
> Just Tantau (p111)
> Firefly (p111)
> 8 Ball (p140)
> Museum of Contemporary Art gift store (p128)
> Wacko (p57)

## COOLEST INDIE STORES
> Amoeba Music (p43)
> Munky King (p130)
> Whimsic Alley (p101)
> Bodhi Tree (p64)

## BEST SHOPPING AVENUES
> Abbot Kinney Blvd (p17)
> Montana Ave (p94)
> Melrose Ave (p64)
> Robertson Blvd (p62)
> 3rd St at La Cienega Blvd (p74)

## OVER-THE-TOP INTERIORS
> Prada (boxed text, p88)
> Harry Winston (p88)
> Whimsic Alley (p101)
> Boule (p65)

**Top left** Designer destination – Rodeo Dr, Beverly Hills (p82)  **Above** Huge and hep Amoeba Music (p43)

# ART SCENE

When you start hearing more buzz about gallery-hopping in Culver City than club-hopping on Hollywood Blvd, it's enough to make you put down your Godiva-chocolate razzmatini. But it's true, LA's art scene is hot on the lips of hipsters and hoi polloi. Long described as 'burgeoning,' LA's artists and galleries have now fully arrived, it seems.

The opening of Santa Monica's Bergamot Station (p95) in 1994 was a big first step. This campus-style complex boasts more than 30 galleries, the Santa Monica Museum of Art and plenty of free parking. Downtown has been the 'it' scene the last few years, riding the crest of a development wave attracting residents, restaurants and bars. The monthly Downtown Art Walk draws connoisseurs and scenesters alike to 27 galleries and museums on the second Thursday of the month (see www.downtownartwalk.com) while exhibits on Chung King Rd lure art-hoppers to Chinatown and its funky late-night bars. Which brings us back to uberfunky Culver City. With 30-odd galleries jostling for attention on S La Cienega and Washington Blvd, this once-industrial neighborhood is enjoying its close-up.

In West Hollywood the Pacific Design Center's 130 showrooms (p64) spotlight architecture and design-minded exhibits, as do galleries along the neighboring Avenues of Art & Design (www.avenuesartdesign.com). Venice marches on with indies – from the sleek LA Louver (p110) to the garage-style trappings of Equator Books (p111). Scan for murals on Venice's Ocean Front Walk (pictured below; p20) and outdoor art near Main St and Rose Ave.

For the latest, check www.artscenecal.com and www.calendarlive.com/galleriesandmuseums. For commentary and links see http://art.blogging.la.

# BEACHES

The stars of *Baywatch, The OC* and *Laguna Beach* weren't the first photogenic faces to inspire waves of California dreamin'. Nope, that would be George Freeth – one part Irish, one part Hawaiian and one part sexy Victorian surf god – who arrived on LA shores 100 years ago with a wooden surfboard to promote Hawaiian tourism. But tycoon and local booster Henry Huntington persuaded young George to stick around, paying him to surf in front of his hotel. Tourists and locals were hooked, and California surf culture was born. Today, surfers head to Malibu's Zuma Beach and Surfrider beaches (boxed text, p104), while South Bay wave hounds check out Manhattan Beach and Hermosa Beach.

But it's not all about the perfect curl. Santa Monica's wide sandy swath is perfect parking for quintessential beach living – volleyball, bodysurfing and tanning are top-notch. Same goes for Manhattan and Hermosa, where the crowds are lighter but it's a bit of a drive to get there. For rambling, Leo Carillo, El Matador and Point Dume offer nature-minded opportunities galore. And free your inner libertarian at Malibu's Surfrider – don't let those giant beach-length fences deter you, just walk through or around them on the sand, as the beaches are private only to the mean high-tide line, no matter what snotty beachside elites would have you to think.

**BEST PEOPLE-WATCHING**
> Venice Beach (p110)
> Manhattan Beach (p118)
> Santa Monica State Beach (p99)

**BEST FOR EXPLORING**
> Leo Carillo (boxed text, p104)
> El Matador (boxed text, p104)
> Malibu (pictured above; boxed text, p104)
> Point Dume (boxed text, p104)

# GAY & LESBIAN LOS ANGELES

Incorporated as its own independent city in 1984, West Hollywood is the center of LA's gay and lesbian population and offers a bit of everything for gay travelers as well as the curious and open-minded. Santa Monica Blvd ('the Boulevard') from Robertson Blvd east to Crescent Heights Blvd is the heart of the weekend scene, as any stroll past the boy brigades spilling out of Here (p67) and Rage (p69) will attest. Check www .visitwesthollywood.com and www.gogaywesthollywood.com for specific theme nights, which vary for buff boys and lipstick ladies.

LA loves a party, and West Hollywood throws some of the best within its 1.9 sq miles. The annual October 31 Halloween Carnaval (pictured below; p29) draws a crowd of 500,000 to the Boulevard. June's LA Gay Pride parade and festival is a two-day celebration of diversity that draws huge crowds to the neighborhood with exhibits and shows (www.lapride.org). The annual AIDS walk draws thousands of fundraisers to the starting line at the Pacific Design Center (p64) for the 6.2-mile trek.

But West Hollywood doesn't hold the key to all the alternative fun. Outfest is one of the largest film festivals in Southern California, with screenings in theatres across town (www.outfest.org). And there are plenty of other gay-friendly neighborhoods beyond WeHo's borders. Silver Lake is known for its lower-key vibe, and its restaurants and bars are more sexually mixed. Santa Monica, Venice, Long Beach and Laguna Beach are the gay-friendliest of the seaside towns.

For additional info see www.weho.org.

# KIDS

Looking around Rodeo Dr, Sunset Strip and downtown's Grand Ave, it's easy to think that LA's children have been banished to a gingerbread cottage in the woods. It's all Cruella De Villes and Baroness von Schraders and nary a ragamuffin in sight. But the kids are here, trust me; you just gotta know where to look.

The term in city planning these days is 'nodes' (art nodes, shopping nodes) – islands of specificity dotting the urban landscape. Kid-friendly nodes include the beaches, where crafty parents can wear out their tykes with bike-riding and body surfing, as well as LA's parks – Griffith (p54) and Will Rogers (boxed text, p55) to name two – where hiking, exploring and animal-watching are top notch. Young Animal Planet devotees can ogle humanesque chimps at Griffith Park's LA Zoo (p55), while future paleontologists can study skeletal saber-toothed cats pulled from the La Brea Tar Pits (p71). At Exposition Park, another node for the stroller-brigade, the Natural History Museum (p129) lures 'em in with exotic stuffed beasts while the California Science Center (p125) boasts keen interactive displays on body works – Digestion! Open-heart surgery! Homeostatis! And of course, don't forget the kiddiest nodes of all, theme parks, with options ranging from all-day happiness at Disneyland (p152) and Universal Studios (p137) to momentary thrills at Pacific Park (p98).

## BEST ANIMAL WATCHING
> LA Zoo (p55)
> Roundhouse Aquarium (p119)
> Santa Monica Pier Aquarium (p98)
> Point Mugu State Park (boxed text, p104)

## BEST OUTDOOR FUN
> LA Zoo (p55) and Griffith Park (p54)
> Leo Carrillo State Park (boxed text, p104)
> Manhattan Beach (p118)
> Santa Monica Pier (p98) and Beach (p99)
> Will Rogers State Park (boxed text, p55)

## BEST KID-FRIENDLY MUSEUMS
> California Science Center (p125)
> Natural History Museum (p129)
> Griffith Observatory (p54)
> Museum of the American West (p56)

## BEST KID-FRIENDLY RESTAURANTS
> Café at the End of the Universe (p59)
> In-n-Out Burger (boxed text, p47)
> Uncle Bill's Pancake House (p122)
> Anywhere at Disneyland (p152)
> Farmers Market at 3rd and Fairfax (p78)

# LITERARY LOS ANGELES

No, that's not an oxymoron. Some may find it hard to believe, but Angelenos like to read. Just ask the 130,000 bibliophiles wandering the booths at the annual LA Festival of Books (p27) every spring. And no, no one's expecting you to hang out in a bookstore while vacationing in LA, but hey, you're reading this book so it's clear you know your way around the stacks. And you never know, you might need something for the beach or the drive up the coast.

LA has its share of chains and some of them are pretty inviting – it's hard to leave the three-story Barnes & Noble at The Grove (p75) empty-handed, and the cosy coffeeshop at the two-story Borders near 3rd St and La Cienega Blvd is perfect for lingering. But it's the indies that really shine. Vroman's Bookstore (p149) in Pasadena is the biggie, with its inviting, customer-centric vibe, while overstuffed Book Soup (p64) on Sunset Strip has an amazing California travel section, not to mention stacks and stacks on cinema and art. For a little conversation and helpful local pointers check out smaller indies like Skylight Books (p57) in Los Feliz or Small World Books (p112) right on the beach in Venice. For specific interest, Larry Edmunds (p44) carries a wide selection of cinema-related tomes, while Equator Books (p111) has all you'll ever need on surfing and architecture. And if you expect a little more from your bookstore than books, try the spiritual-minded Bodhi Tree (p64), where psychics will tell you your future, or Distant Lands (p149), where jaunty caps await if your future holds a hike to Mt Hollywood's summit.

## BEST BOOKSTORE CATS
> Skylight Books (p57)
> Small World Books (p112)

## BEST LARGE INDIE BOOKSTORES
> Vroman's Bookstore (p149)
> Book Soup (p64)

## BEST BOOKSTORE FOR MENTAL TRAVEL
> Bodhi Tree (p64)

## BEST BOOKSTORES FOR PHYSICAL TRAVEL
> Distant Lands Travel Bookstore & Outfitters (p149)
> Travelers Bookcase (p77)
> Small World Books (p112)
> Skylight Books (p57)

# LIVE MUSIC

Yeah, Sheryl Crow may wanna have some fun 'til the sun comes up over Santa Monica Blvd, but you know what's more fun? Watching the sun go down on the Hollywood Hills, particularly from the back benches of the Hollywood Bowl (p51). The $1 cheap seats are made for kickin' back, taking up space and absorbing an awesome mash-up of music, nature and community. From the LA Phil to Lyle Lovett to Sheryl Crow herself, there's no bad seat in the house. Speaking of the LA Phil, the only place better than the Bowl to hear classical music is the acoustically superb Walt Disney Concert Hall (p129). But one man's sublime is another man's snooze, and headbangers might prefer mixing it up on the Sunset Strip where old faves like the Roxy (pictured below), Whisky-a-Go-Go and the Viper Room rock on for the faithful. The young and the rowdy – and those who have all day to sleep – should head east to Hollywood Blvd and the Cahuenga Corridor for the newest, most energized late-night clubs. Jazz fans can check out the cool grooves of Hollywood's Catalina Bar & Grill (p49) or the funkier sounds of Santa Monica's rowdy Harvelle's (p107). One of LA's smallest venues packs the biggest punch – Hollywood's Hotel Café (p51), a friendly little outfit catering mainly to acoustic up-and-comers in a low-key respite, seemingly miles from the scene-splashed Cahuenga surroundings. Check club websites before you arrive or skim www.calendarlive.com.

### BEST SMALL VENUES FOR SINGER-SONGWRITERS
> Hotel Café (p51)
> McCabe's Guitar Shop (p107)
> Amoeba Music (p43)
> Troubadour (p69)

### BEST OUTDOOR CONCERTS
> Hollywood Bowl (p51)
> Greek Theatre (p61)
> Ford Amphitheatre (p51)

# MOVIE VIEWING

'The cinema is the greatest means of expression ever invented,' pronounced legendary director King Vidor, 'but it is an illusion more powerful than any other and it should therefore be in the hands of the magicians and wizards who can bring it to life.' Well put, and once brought to life, the movie-viewing experience should be magical too.

For those weary of tiny screens, sticky floors and uninterested teens at their neighborhood multiplex, give movie night another shot while visiting LA. With just the right movie at just the right cinema, you might be reminded that big-screen escapism is often the best chicken soup for the psyche. Historic Hollywood, with its 1920s-era movie palaces, boasts some of the finest theaters in town. For current releases, nothing charms more than Grauman's Chinese Theatre (p39), with its footprint-filled courtyard, palatial lobby and exquisite viewing hall. A few blocks away shines state-of-the-art ArcLight Cinemas (p48), a modern movie house with new millennium pluses – preselected seats, no late entry, and a well-stocked bar for theater-bound thirsty. But theaters aren't the only option – get a full cultural immersion at a LACMA screening or a mood-drenched outdoor show at Hollywood Forever Cemetery (p39).

Hankering for true legends? Try The Silent Movie Theatre (www.silentmovietheatre.com) in Mid-City or the ongoing screenings of classics by American Cinematheque at Hollywood's Egyptian Theatre (p50) and Santa Monica's Aero (www.americancinematheque.com). Who knows, you might catch a favorite director or actress attending a retrospective Q&A. Indies and cult faves pack 'em in at Laemmle's Sunset 5 (www.laemmle.com) and the New Beverly (www.newbevcinema.com). Good sources are www.calendarlive.com and www.laweekly.com.

### BEST FOR RETROSPECTIVES

> Aero Theatre (www.american cinematheque.com)
> Egyptian Theatre (p50)
> Los Angeles County Museum of Art (p71)
> UCLA Film and TV Archive at the Hammer Museum (p86)

### MOST MEMORABLE THEATERS

> Egyptian Theatre (p50)
> Grauman's Chinese Theatre (p39)
> Cinerama Dome at ArcLight Cinemas (p48)
> Hollywood Forever Cemetery (p39)

# OUTDOOR ADVENTURE

With bike paths, mountain trails, pounding surf and wind-blown seas minutes away, the question isn't whether you should enjoy the outdoors, but how. Possibilities for adventure are almost endless; just ask the parade of bikers, surfers and boat owners hustling past for their daily outdoor fix.

Hollywood visitors short on time can zip a loop around Runyon Canyon (boxed text, p55) northwest of La Brea Ave where a steep uphill climb, great views, and a no-leash policy lures Hollywood hipsters and their pooches. Griffith Park (p54) boasts 53 miles of trails plus the iconic hike to the summit of Mt Hollywood (*not* the location of the sign), where stellar 360-degree views await, smog-willing. Tree-lined trails along the coastal mountains give it up for ocean and canyon fans, while bikers bounce over the Backbone Trail on the southern spine of the Santa Monicas near Will Rogers State Park (boxed text, p55). Beach cruisers may prefer the flat 22-mile South Bay Bicycle Path from Will Rogers State Beach to within a spoke of Palos Verdes.

Don't like exercising alone? John Muir's 110-year-old Sierra Club lets nonmembers join its organized, very welcoming hikes and bike rides, geared to various fitness levels. See www.angeles.sierraclub.org to choose from hundreds. The night hikes are especially cool. Mountain-bikers should check www.corbamtb.com and www.socalmtb.com for conditions.

Trust me, a short mountain hike or beachside bike ride will be one of your most memorable LA encounters. Other than bumping into that girl from *Dancing with the Stars*.

### BEST SHORT HIKES WITH VIEWS
> Charlie Turner Trail to
  Mt Hollywood (boxed text, p55)
> Inspiration Point (boxed text, p55)
> Temescal Canyon Loop Hike (boxed
  text, p55)
> Runyon Canyon (right; boxed text, p55)

### BEST EASE-OF-ACCESS BIKING
> Backbone Trail near Will Rogers State
  Park (boxed text, p55)
> South Bay Bicycle Trail (p99)
> Griffith Park (p54)

# TRAFFIC

Bringing up traffic in a travel guide may be akin to discussing *E coli* at a backyard barbecue, but if your burger's half-cooked, someone's gonna be unhappy down the road. Likewise, if you drive in LA, you can avoid unhappiness with the right knowledge and preparation.

First, check www.sigalert.com for traffic updates. A sigalert is any traffic problem expected to tie up two or more freeway lanes for two or more hours. Avoid driving east on the I-10 (pictured below; Santa Monica Fwy) after 4pm. Unless you have a full gas tank and several spare hours, don't do it. If you have tickets for the Walt Disney Concert Hall, you'll probably be late. Plan to leave Westside early in the afternoon then wander the Fashion District, Chinatown or MOCA until showtime.

Other points? The I-405 (San Diego Fwy) and the I-101 (Hollywood Fwy) can become sluggish almost instantly, even in the middle of the day. Also know that there are stoplights on many freeway entrance ramps to regulate traffic flow. Obey them. Sunset Strip on weekend nights is a cruising nightmare. Finally, most stoplights don't have left-hand turn signals so drivers have to turn left on a red light. Two is the acceptable (but maybe not legal) number of cars that can turn left on red. Oncoming traffic knows to wait. Now you do too. And if traffic happens anyway? Just treat the experience like an LA highlight: 'Oh my gawd…I saw Lindsay Lohan at Kitson and then I bought these totally bitchin' Uggs at The Grove, and then, check this out, I got stuck in this rockin' sigalert on the 405. We didn't move for three hours, it was off the chain.' See? It's all in the spin and the attitude.

# >BACKGROUND

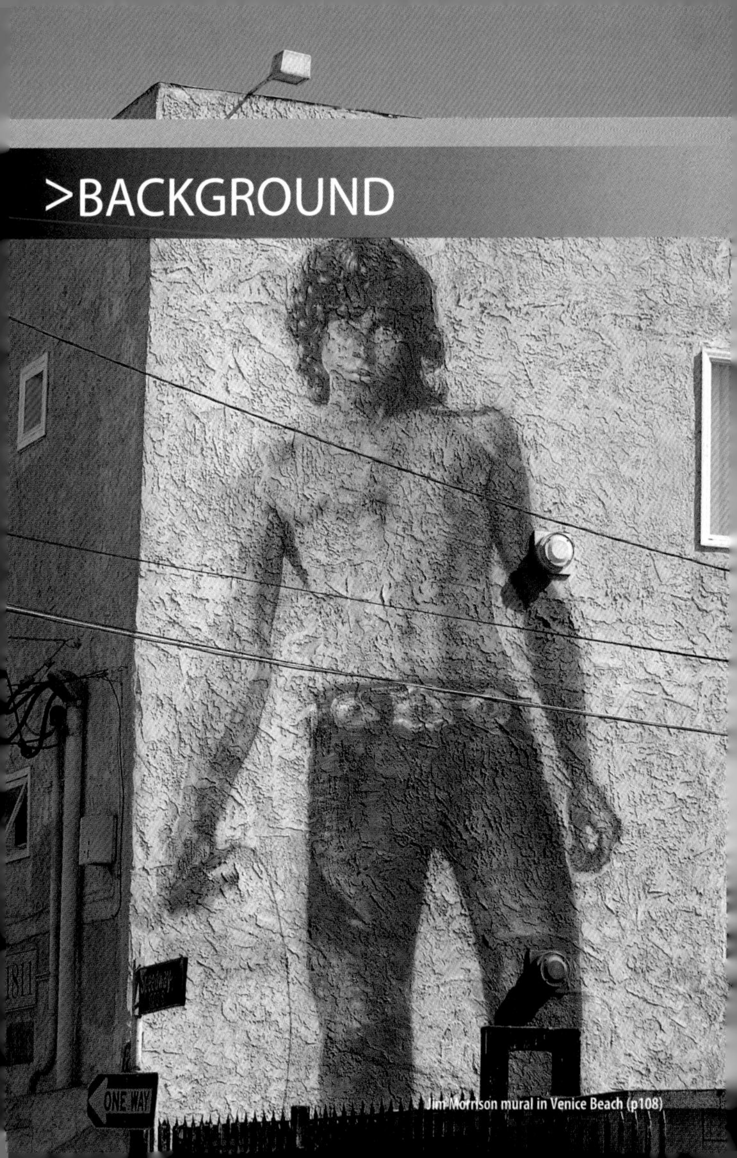


Jim Morrison mural in Venice Beach (p108)

# BACKGROUND
## HISTORY
### SPANISH SETTLEMENT

The coastal Chumash and Gabrielino tribes inhabited the region for thousands of years, living a relatively peaceful existence as hunter-gatherers until the arrival of Spanish explorers and missionaries in the late 1700s. Pursuant to King Carlos III's directive to establish missionaries and agricultural outposts in Alta (Upper) California, Gaspar de Tortola led a Spanish expedition through the area in 1769, traveling north from Baja, California, and eventually wandering west along a footpath now known as Wilshire Blvd.

Mission San Gabriel, the fourth in what would become a chain of 21 missions, was established in 1771 under the guidance of Father Junipero Serra. Mission life was no great salvation for the Indians in the ensuing years; many of them suffered abuses at the hands of the soldiers and caught European diseases such as smallpox and syphilis. In 1781 a tiny band of settlers left the mission, traveling 9 miles west to set up an agricultural community near the river. This isolated village, known as El Pueblo de la Reina de Los Angeles – the Town of the Queen of Angels – became a thriving farming community.

### INCORPORATION

In 1821 Mexico won independence from Spain and the missions were soon secularized. Mexican governors granted large swaths of land, or 'ranchos,' to worthy soldiers and citizens. The first overland settlers arrived in Los Angeles in 1841, a trickle before the flood that followed President James Polk's rallying cry for America's Manifest Destiny and the settling of the West. Following this lead, the US declared, fought and won a war with Mexico between 1846 and 1848, taking claim to LA and the rest of California. Pushed along by the booming Gold Rush scene in San Francisco, California was declared America's 31st state in 1850. That same year, Los Angeles was incorporated.

In the ensuing years, many rancheros lost their land as the American government questioned their title under the 1851 Land Act. During this loose governmental period, LA was a true Wild West town, filled with saloons, brothels and gambling dens. Added to the mix were thousands of Chinese immigrants who'd arrived for the gold rush and railroad work.

These foreigners were viewed by many with suspicion. Suspicion turned to hostility in 1871 during the Chinese Massacre when a local mob took the law into its own hands and murdered 19 Chinese men and boys following the death of a white citizen caught in the crossfire of a dispute in the Chinese community.

The perception of the city as a lawless backwater began to change in 1876 when the first Southern Pacific train arrived from San Francisco, followed by the Santa Fe Railroad less than a decade later. City boosters began marketing Los Angeles as a sunny paradise, and wealthy Midwesterners heeded the sirens' call, traveling by train to LA and Pasadena to escape the hard winters. Many of them decided to settle here permanently, drawn by the weather and perceived health benefits. At the same time, the success of orange groves and oil fields was pushing the economy forward, and the *Los Angeles Times*, led by publisher Harrison Gray Otis, was leading the boosterism charge.

## A GROWING CITY

There were a number of important firsts for the city in the ensuing decades. The first car appeared on LA streets in 1897, Irish-Hawaiian George Freeth first surfed California waves in 1907 to admiring crowds, and in 1910 spectators looked to the skies for America's first aviation show – where the planes actually flew – north of Long Beach.

Important developments were unfolding behind the scenes too. Division of Water & Power (DWP) chief William Mulholland and other city business leaders realized that still-growing Los Angeles would need water beyond that found in the LA River. Deciding that a 233-mile aqueduct carrying snow-fed waters from Owens Valley would do the trick, the men secretly began buying up property in Owens Valley under false pretenses, only going public once enough water rights and land parcels were secured. The project was completed in 1913 and development surged ahead, buffeted by newfound water now pouring into the city. LA began its march to national prominence while the formerly fertile Owens Valley became a dusty, barren wasteland.

Entrepreneurial movie-makers – most of them European immigrants – were establishing the city's first great movie studios at this time. German-born Carl Laemmle built Universal Studios in 1915, selling lunch to curious guests come to watch the magic of movie-making. Polish immigrant Samuel Goldwyn joined with Cecil B DeMille and others to form Paramount Studios. Jack Warner and his brothers arrived a few years later.

With the perpetually sunny weather, most outdoor locations could be easily shot, and movie-making flourished. Fans loved early film stars like Charlie Chaplin and Harold Lloyd, and the first 'big' Hollywood wedding occurred in 1920 when Douglas Fairbanks wed Mary Pickford. Hollywood hit its stride in the 1920s as the glamorous movie palaces opened their doors along Hollywood Blvd.

LA's hubris was on full display by the end of the decade, with both inspiring and disastrous effects. The 32-story City Hall was completed in 1928 – an eye-catching, chest-thumping skyscraper towering above the downtown skyline, a bold exception to the earthquake-conscious height limitations imposed on other downtown buildings. That same year, the St Francis dam, constructed 45 miles north of LA under the hurried, careless watch of Chief Mulholland, collapsed, and the resulting rush of water killed more than 400 people.

This odd mix of reckless disregard and unfettered rah-rah continued into the Depression years. Not only were LA police officers regularly loading Hispanics onto trains and deporting them, they also at one point physically prevented Dust Bowl refugees from entering the state. In the same decade, however, LA created Olvera St, a shopping and dining destination downtown that celebrated Hispanic heritage, and welcomed the world to the 1932 Olympics. Media darlings at the time included the madcap gymnasts at Santa Monica's Muscle Beach and Hollywood's Shirley Temple, who was tap-dancing her way into the hearts of millions.

But LA had more cause to tap-dance than the rest of the country. The aviation industry had been booming since WWI when the Lockheed brothers and Donald Douglas established aircraft manufacturing plants in LA. By the 1930s the aviation industry, helped along by billions of federal dollars for military contracts, helped lift LA out of the Great Depression.

## WWII TO TODAY

The deluge of new residents arriving after WWII, not to mention the construction of 160-plus miles of freeways, drove LA forward, shaping it into the megalopolis it is today. Unconstrained growth, however, brought attendant problems including suburban sprawl, air pollution and racial strife. Major riots in 1965 and 1992, as well as a police corruption scandal in the 1990s, created an abyss of distrust between the police department and various ethnic groups.

Beginning in the late 1990s, though, civic pride returned as dynamic new buildings – the Getty Center, the Staples Center, Our Lady of the Angels Cathedral, Walt Disney Concert Hall – cropped up all over the LA landscape. Energy and buzz, not to mention condos and upscale residents, returned to downtown and Hollywood, and new restaurants, bars and businesses are still eager to join the scene. Violent crime has dropped under the watch of new police Chief William Bratton, who arrived in 2002 from New York, and in May 2005 the city elected Antonio Villaraigosa, its first Latino mayor since 1872. Although pollution, traffic and soaring real-estate prices are continuing problems, the economy remains strong, and unemployment and crime rates remain low. And the sun still shines 300 days out of the year.

# LIFE AS AN ANGELENO

Just who lives in LA? If you believe the stereotypes, they're a flaky bunch. Liberal. Self-absorbed. Greedy. Botoxed and blow-dried. Though these adjectives may have a hint of truth for certain subgroups, with four million people crammed into the city's 465 square miles and 10 million jostling for space in sprawling LA County, no one label fits all. Statistically, the county's divided about 50/50 male/female with Hispanics comprising 47% of the population, non-Hispanic whites 30%, blacks almost 10% and Asian 13%.

How is this diversity playing out in the early 21st century? Simmering issues of distrust linger between various communities but day-to-day life isn't quite as bleak as portrayed in Paul Haggis' 2005 Oscar-winning *Crash*. The main problem? People are quick to demand respect but slow to give it out. The town also runs high on false friendliness and let's-do-lunch superficiality; there's a bit more 'I' and 'me' than 'we' and 'us.' This attitude is displayed at its worst in the car culture. Freeways and surface streets are perpetually jammed with solo SUV drivers heading to the gym to workout, to the two-blocks-away grocery store and even Sierra Club meetings. Are we interested in carpooling to work? Mmm, not so much.

But Angelenos aren't all bad. Optimism, open-mindedness and outside-the-box thinking are the norm (studio execs excluded), and people tend to work hard. From illegal immigrants on the corner ready for a long day's work to downtown office workers earning overtime for ballooning mortgage payments to Hollywood assistants holding dreary day jobs while cramming free hours with indie projects, everybody's hustling.

BACKGROUND

Griffith Park might be in flames, the Hollywood Hills crumbling and the ground shaking under our feet, but if it's not blocking traffic, get out of the way. Yes, our reach may sometimes exceed our grasp, but isn't that what LA's for?

## DOS & DON'TS

Los Angeles – led by the omnipresent mores of the entertainment industry – is pretty laid-back when it comes to socially acceptable behavior. In fact, if all the city's sociopaths, narcissists and foul-mouthed 'geniuses' were asked to leave the city tomorrow, we wouldn't have anything to watch on TV or the big screen. Fashion-wise, jeans and flip-flops really are acceptable just about anywhere at anytime, although you may want to spruce up just a bit for business meetings and some of the posher restaurants.

Don't litter or jaywalk, especially in nicer neighborhoods where you may be fined if caught. Keep your dogs on a leash at all times outdoors, and be sure to clean up after them. Smoking is prohibited in all public places, including the beaches of Santa Monica. At the beach, be sure to watch the signs for the beachside bike and pedestrian paths – some are designated for use solely by one or the other. When roller-blading and cycling, stick to the right-hand side of the road or path. As a courtesy and safety measure, let those ahead know if you're passing – especially if it's at high speed.

To avoid incurring the wrath of surfers, don't drop in on a wave already being surfed by another. On the freeways, drive defensively and don't cut off other drivers, follow too close or honk your horn excessively.

# ENVIRONMENT

LA's infamous smog has hovered over Los Angeles for centuries, first mentioned historically by Spanish explorer Juan Rodriguez Cabrillo in the 1540s after he observed 'many smokes' from Native American campfires hanging over the LA Bay. Today, smog is a yellowish-brown layer of toxic fumes that's an unwanted by-product of car and factory emissions. Ozone levels peak during summer when a layer of warm air traps the noxious fumes. Despite the ongoing problem, the number of annual days exceeding health-standard levels has dropped since the 1970s after the implementation of tougher environmental regulations.

Run-off pollution from the city's drains continues to pollute the bay after big storms, and surfers and beachgoers alike are advised to stay away until the water clears. Speaking of water, 85% of it is delivered to the city via aqueducts from far outside the city. This dependency, not to mention decreases in the water-supplying snow packs on the distant mountains, will likely be a major issue in the not-too-distant future.

But Californians are generally ecofriendly in nature – even Governor Arnold Schwarzenegger has switched from driving monstrous gas-guzzling Humvees to hydrogen and biodiesel versions – and will continue to lead the nation, if not the world, in the development of environmentally sound technologies.

# FURTHER READING

Though written in 1939, Nathanael West's novel *The Day of the Locust* is still considered the classic skewering of the excesses of Hollywood. F Scott Fitzgerald, who spent his last years working as a Hollywood screenwriter, provides an inspired, though unfinished, take on the rise of MGM studio head Irving Thalberg in the 1940 novel *The Last Tycoon*. Budd Schulberg followed a year later with his novel about ruthless go-getter Sammy Glick in *What Makes Sammy Run?*

Novelist Raymond Chandler set the standard for hard-boiled detectives with his tough-talking Philip Marlowe who sought truth in seedy Bay City, a thinly veiled stand-in for Santa Monica, in *The Big Sleep* and *Farewell, My Lovely*. Walter Mosley's *Devil in a Blue Dress*, James Ellroy's *Black Dahlia* and Elmore Leonard's *Get Shorty* continue the LA-as-crime-scene tradition.

Charles Bukowski's *Post Office*, Joan Didion's *Play It as It Lays* and Bret Easton Ellis' *Less than Zero* offer insightful, harsh, but always fascinating appraisals of the city's varied denizens.

# CINEMA & TELEVISION

One of the best films to examine Tinseltown's one-of-a-kind combination of ego, insecurity and ambition also is one of the oldest: Preston Sturgis' 1941 comedic *Sullivan's Travels*. Billy Wilder's 1950 *Sunset Boulevard* takes a darker view of the perils of stardom while Robert Altman's satiric *The Player* and Elmore Leonard's quirky *Get Shorty* offer more recent, but still cutting, analyses of movie-making.

Inspired by short stories by Raymond Carver, Robert Altman's *Short Cuts* is a sprawling movie with interlocking tales that capture the moody angst of the characters and the city in the early 1990s. Other films skill-fully interweaving the lives of Angelenos include Paul Thomas Anderson's take on the 1970s porn industry, *Boogie Nights,* as well as his Aimee Mann–inspired vision of characters passing in the night, and occasionally connecting, at the end of the millennium in *Magnolia*. Paul Haggis' *Crash*, winner of the 2005 Oscar for Best Picture, examines the simmering, sometimes explosive, differences between the city's various ethnic subcultures.

For cops and robbers with a taste of noir, check out Roman Polanski's classic *Chinatown*, Curtis Hanson's moody *LA Confidential* or Ridley Scott's futuristic *Blade Runner*. LA seems to be its own separate character in a number of films: a stylish lurker in Michael Mann's *Heat* and *Collateral*, a stark aggressor in Antoine Fuqua's *Training Day*, and an over-the-top eccentric in Quentin Tarantino's *Pulp Fiction*.

There's plenty of offbeat and upbeat viewing, too. From goofy but insightful teen romps like *Fast Times at Ridgemont High* and *Clueless* to quirky city odes like *LA Story* and *Swingers*, it's nice to be reminded that no one should ever take LA too seriously.

As for TV, the babes, beaches and surfboards of *Baywatch* captivated viewers worldwide in the '90s, as did the glamorized teens of *Beverly Hills 90210*. The tradition continued into the new millennium with the rich but trouble-prone teens of *The OC*. Today, HBO's *Entourage* is a perfect pre-trip primer that takes a comedic but accurate-at-the-heart look at everyday life for LA's young, beautiful and rich and those that hover near them. 'Reality' shows *Laguna Beach* and *The Hills* draw millions of viewers, proving that stories about good-looking teens and the beach will always do well. And last but certainly not least is cultural steamroller *American Idol*. Taped in LA, this king of all reality shows encourages wannabe pop stars to sing their way to stardom, its off-the-charts ratings proving that stories of everyday people chasing their dreams still captivate American audiences.

# DIRECTORY
## TRANSPORTATION
### ARRIVAL & DEPARTURE
**AIR**

**Los Angeles International Airport** (LAX; ☎ 310-646-5252; www.lawa.org/lax) is about 17 miles southwest of downtown, bounded by the Pacific Ocean to the west and the San Diego Fwy (I-405) to the east.

There are nine terminals in the U-shaped complex, including the Tom Bradley international terminal located at the base of the U. The terminals are accessible by car on two levels, the upper used for departures and the lower for arrivals.

Foreign currency exchange and ATMs are found in every terminal.

Hotel and car-rental information kiosks are located in or adjacent to baggage claim as are **Travelers Aid information booths** ( ☎ 310-646-2270). **Cell phones** ( ☎ 310-645-3500) can be rented on the lower level of the international terminal.

A **first aid station** ( ☎ 310-215-6000; ☉ 10am-10pm) can be found on the upper level of the international terminal. In case of an emergency, call **airport police** ( ☎ 310-646-7911).

Terminal maps are available at www.lawa.org/lax/terminalmap .cfm.

Mid-sized LA airports include Burbank's **Bob Hope Airport** (Map pp138-9, C1; BUR; ☎ 818-840-8840; www .burbankairport.com) and **Long Beach Airport** (LGB; ☎ 562-570-2600; www .longbeach.gov/airport).

---

### CLIMATE CHANGE & TRAVEL

Travel – especially air travel – is a significant contributor to global climate change. At Lonely Planet, we believe that all who travel have a responsibility to limit their personal impact. As a result, we have teamed with Rough Guides and other concerned industry partners to support Climate Care, which allows people to offset the greenhouse gases they are responsible for with contributions to energy-saving projects and other climate-friendly initiatives in the developing world. Lonely Planet offsets all staff and author travel.

For more information, turn to the responsible travel pages on www.lonelyplanet .com. For details on offsetting your carbon emissions and a carbon calculator, go to www .climatecare.org.

There are alternatives to flying to LA, and to driving once you're there. One of SoCal's most scenic modes of travel is Amtrak's *Pacific Surfliner*. Although she may be more of a chugging old faithful than a sleek silver bullet, the Surfliner does provide stress-free, big-windowed views of the land and sea between San Luis Obispo and San Diego. And within LA the metro is a smart, low-cost and speedy option for travel between downtown and Pasadena as well as between Hollywood and Universal Studios.

## TRAIN

**Amtrak** ( ☎ 800-872-7245; www.amtrak
.com), America's national rail
service, rolls into downtown Los
Angeles at historic **Union Station**
(Map pp126-7, F3; 800 N Alameda St). The
*Pacific Surfliner* travels daily to
San Diego ($29, 2¾ hours), Santa
Barbara ($21, 2½ hours) and San
Luis Obispo ($30, 5½ hours) from
Union Station. Cross-country trains
departing Union Station include
the scenic, but not necessarily
timely, *Coast Starlight*, *Southwest
Chief* and *Sunset Limited*.

## BUS

**Greyhound** ( ☎ 800-231-2222; www.grey
hound.com) operates extensive, if
slow, routes across North America.
Its main Los Angeles terminal is
**downtown** (Map pp126-7, E6; ☎ 213-629-
8401; 1716 E 7th St). Other terminals
include **Hollywood** (Map pp40-1, E3;
☎ 323-466-6381; 1715 N Cahuenga Blvd)
and **Pasadena** (Map pp146-7, E2; ☎ 626-
792-5116; 645 E Walnut St).

## TRAVEL DOCUMENTS

Since the rules for entry into the
US are constantly changing, check
with the United States Consulate in
your home country for up-to-date
information as well as the visa
website of the US Department of
State (www.unitedstatesvisas.gov;
www.travel.state.gov/visa) and
the travel section of US Customs &
Border Protection (www.cbp.gov).

Under the US Visa Waiver
Program, visas are currently
not required for citizens of 27
countries for stays up to 90 days
(no extensions allowed) as long
as they have a machine-readable
passport (MRP). If you don't have
an MRP, you will need a visa to
enter the USA.

If you're getting a new passport,
note the requirements are even
tighter. Under current regulations,
passports issued between October
26, 2005 and October 25, 2006
must be machine readable and
feature a digital photograph on
the data page. Passports issued
after October 25, 2006 must be
machine readable and also include
an integrated chip with biometric
information from the data pages.

If you have a passport issued
before October 26, 2005, it will still
be accepted for travel as long as it's
machine readable. In other words,
there's no need to get a new passport until your current one expires.

Canadian citizens are techni-
cally exempt from both visa and
passport requirements but official
proof of citizenship with photo
is necessary. Valid documents
include a birth certificate, a citizenship certificate or passport.

Citizens from all non-visa-
waiver countries need to apply for
a visa in their home country. The
process may take some time, so
apply as early as possible.

## GETTING AROUND

In this book, the nearest metro station Ⓜ or bus route Ⓑ is noted before each review.

### TRAVEL PASSES

The **Metro Transit Authority** (MTA; ☎ 800-266-6883, TTD 800-252-9040; www.mta.net) operates about 200 bus lines as well as the four Metro Rail lines. The MTA sells day ($3) and weekly ($14) passes, valid on both its buses and rail lines. Tickets and passes are sold at more than 600 retail outlets around town, and at MTA customer centers including **Union Station** (Map pp126-7, F3; ☀ 6am-6:30pm Mon-Fri) and **Mid-City** (Map pp72-3, E5; 5301 Wilshire Blvd; ☀ 9am-5pm Mon-Fri).

### BUS

A network of bus routes spans the metropolis, with most operated by **Metro Transit Authority** (MTA; ☎ 800-266-6883, TTD 800-252-9040; www.mta.net). Its one-way fare is $1.25 ($0.75 after 9pm) and up to $2.25 for freeway routes. Most routes operate 5am to 2am daily. Individual tickets and day passes (exact fare required) can be purchased from the bus driver.

Fast, frequent Metro Rapid buses (numbered in the 700s) make limited stops. Bus 720 travels downtown from Santa Monica via Westwood, Beverly Hills and

Mid-City's Miracle Mile along Wilshire in about 45 to 90 minutes depending on departure time.

### DASH MINIBUSES

For quick hops, **DASH minibuses** (☎ 800-266-6883; www.ladottransit.com) cost just $0.25. Six downtown DASH routes, A to F, run every five to 20 minutes from 6:30am to 6:30pm or 7pm weekdays with limited service on weekends. Other key DASH routes for visitors include Fairfax, Hollywood and Hollywood/West Hollywood.

### BIG BLUE BUS

Santa Monica's **Big Blue Bus** (☎ 310-451-5444; www.bigbluebus.com) rumbles through much of western LA including Beverly Hills, Culver City, Westwood/UCLA and Venice. One-way fares are $0.75 and transfers to a different bus system are $0.25. The freeway express to downtown LA costs $1.75 (from another bus, transfer is $1). Big Blue Bus routes are abbreviated 'BBB' in this book's reviews. The Tide Shuttle ($0.25) departs Santa Monica Pl at Third St Promenade for Venice Beach via Ocean Ave, returning north via Main St every 15 minutes from noon to 8pm (to 10pm Friday and Saturday).

### METRO RAIL

Operated by MTA, Metro Rail light-rail trains connect downtown with

## Transport to/from LAX

| | Taxi | City bus | Metro board 'G' shuttle |
|---|---|---|---|
| **Pickup point** | lower level curbside | lower level under blue sign 'LAX Shuttle & Airline Connections' | lower level under blue sign 'LAX Shuttle & Airline Connections' |
| **Drop-off point** | confirm with driver | LA County Metropolitan Transportation Authority Bus Center | LA County Metropolitan Transportation Authority Metro Green Line Aviation Station |
| **Duration** | to downtown, 45min-2hr, depending on traffic; to Santa Monica 20-30min | 10min | 5-10min |
| **Cost** | to Santa Monica $20-25; to Beverly Hills $25-30; to downtown $35-40 | shuttle C to bus center free; MTA bus one-way $1.25, unlimited daypass $3 | shuttle G to Metro Center free; MTA metro one-way $1.25, unlimited daypass $3 |
| **Other** | ticket stating standard fares should be provided | MTA buses as well as Culver City buses & Santa Monica's Big Blue Bus stop at bus center | better to use Flyaway Shuttle or city buses than metro from LAX |
| **Contact** | see below | www.metro.net (or www.mta .net); www.ladottransit.com | www.metro.net |

Hollywood and Universal City (Red Line), Pasadena (Gold Line), LAX (Green Line) and Long Beach (Blue Line). One-way fares are $1.25. Trains run approximately 5am to midnight.

### TAXI
Most companies charge a $2.20 base fee then $2.20 per mile. Don't expect to hail a cab from the sidewalk; you need to call ahead. Try **Bell Cab** ( ☎ 888-235-5222), **Checker Cab** ( ☎ 800-300-5007) or **Yellow Cab** ( ☎ 800-200-1085). Costs can add up quickly in traffic-snarled LA. Surcharges for airport drop-offs,

pick-ups and extra passengers and luggage may also apply.

### CAR & MOTORCYCLE
If you're planning to visit several neighborhoods, it may be wise to rent a car. Because of LA's sprawl, public transportation can be cumbersome and time-consuming, while taxis can be prohibitively expensive. Embracing LA's carcentric mentality will be easier on your patience if not your conscience. Rental rates start at about $20 a day or $120 a week for unlimited mileage, exclusive of taxes and insurance. Surcharges

| Hotel shuttles | Commercial shuttles | Downtown Flyaway shuttle |
| --- | --- | --- |
| lower level under red sign 'Hotel & Parking Lot Shuttles' | lower level under orange sign 'Shared Ride Vans' | lower level under green sign 'Flyaway, Buses & Long Distance Vans' |
| area hotels & private parking garages | check with companies, but typically as requested | Union Station (downtown) |
| varies | varies | 45min |
| check with hotel for costs & discounts | to Santa Monica around $14; to downtown around $15; to Hollywood around $24 | $3 |
| confirm details with hotel | confirm details with company | departs every 30min 5am-1am, every hour on the hour 1am-5am |
| check with individual hotels | www.supershuttle.com; www.primetimeshuttle.com | www.lawa.org/flyawayinfo2.cfm |

for airport rental fees, additional drivers and one-way rentals can increase the price by a sometimes shocking amount. Secure a low price via the internet or phone in advance, usually with no cancellation penalty, before walking up cold to the rental counter.

Compare prices at www.kayak.com, www.orbitz.com and www.expedia.com or check company websites directly. Rental car companies at LAX include the following:
**Alamo** ( ☎ 800-327-9633; www.alamo.com)
**Avis** ( ☎ 800-331-1212; www.avis.com)
**Budget** ( ☎ 800-527-0700; www.budget.com)

**Dollar** ( ☎ 800-800-4000; www.dollar.com)
**Enterprise** ( ☎ 800-325-8007; www.enterprise.com)
**Hertz** ( ☎ 800-654-3131; www.hertz.com)
**National** ( ☎ 800-227-7368; www.nationalcar.com)
**Thrifty** ( ☎ 800-367-2277; www.thrifty.com)

LA's freeways are variously referred to by number or by name. To add to the fun, the same freeway may have a different name in a different region. Here are the biggies:
**I-5** Golden State/Santa Ana Fwy
**I-10** Santa Monica/San Bernardino Fwy
**I-110** Pasadena/Harbor Fwy

## Transportation Within LA

| | Burbank | Downtown | Hollywood |
|---|---|---|---|
| **Burbank** | | Metro red line 20min | Metro red line 4min |
| **Downtown** | Metro red line 20min | | Metro red line 15min |
| **Hollywood** | Metro red line 4min | Metro red line 15min | |
| **LAX** | car 1hr | Flyaway shuttle 45min-1hr | car 45min-1hr |
| **Long Beach** | car 1hr-90min | Metro blue line 53min | car 90min |
| **Pasadena** | car 30min | Metro gold line 25min | car 35-45min |
| **Santa Monica** | car 1hr | Big Blue Bus 10 40-90min | car 45min-1hr |

**I-405** San Diego Fwy
**I-710** Long Beach Fwy
**US 101** Hollywood/Ventura Fwy
**Hwy 1** Pacific Coast Hwy (PCH)

Freeways should be avoided during rush hour (5am to 9am and 3pm to 7pm), although traffic jams can occur at any time. Beachfront highways get jammed on weekend mornings, and Sunset Strip is slow going on weekend nights.

On-street parking can be tight. If you find a spot, it may be metered or restricted, so obey posted signs to avoid a ticket. Private lots and parking garages cost at least $5 a day and can be much more expensive downtown. Valet parking can cost as much as $30 a day. Municipal lots near Rodeo Dr in Beverly Hills and bordering Third St Promenade in Santa Monica are free for a certain time.

### Driver's License

Visitors can legally drive in California with a valid driver's license issued in their home country. If your license is not in English, you may be required to show an international driving permit (IDP), which may also be required when renting a car, especially if your home license is not in English or if it doesn't have a photograph. To obtain an IDP, stop by your local automobile association with a passport photo and home license. Be sure to carry both while driving.

# PRACTICALITIES
## BUSINESS HOURS

Normal business hours are 9am to 5pm Monday to Friday. Banks usually open from 8:30am to 4:30pm Monday to Thursday and to 5:30pm Friday; some also open

| LAX | Long Beach | Pasadena | Santa Monica |
| --- | --- | --- | --- |
| car 1hr | car 1hr-90min | car 30min | car 1hr |
| Flyaway shuttle 45min-1hr | Metro blue line 53min | Metro gold line 25min | Big Blue Bus 10 40-90min |
| car 45min-1hr | car 90min | car 35-45min | car 45min-1hr |
| | car 45min | car 40min-1hr | car 20-30min |
| car 45min | | car 45min | car 45min |
| car 40min-1hr | car 45min | | car 40min |
| car 20-30min | car 45min | car 40min | |

from 9am to 2pm Saturday. Post offices are open from 9am to 6pm weekdays, and some also open 9am to 2pm on Saturday. Shops open from 10am to 6pm Monday to Saturday, though shopping malls may close later, and noon to 5pm Sunday. Bars are generally late afternoon until 2am.

Restaurants generally serve lunch from 11am to 2:30pm and dinner from 5:30pm to 10pm.

There are a fair number of 24-hour supermarkets, convenience stores, gas stations and diners. Banks, schools and government offices (including post offices) are closed on major holidays (see right), while museums, public transport and other services may use a Sunday schedule. Businesses may close on July 4, Thanksgiving, Christmas Day and New Year's Day.

## EMERGENCIES

During earthquakes, stand under a sturdy doorframe and protect your head with your arms until tremors subside. Violent crime is mostly confined to well-defined areas of East LA and South LA, as well as less-trafficked blocks in Hollywood, Venice and down-town. Avoid these areas after dark. Downtown is the site of 'Skid Row,' an area roughly bounded by 3rd, Alameda, 7th and Main, where many of the city's homeless spend the night.

**Police, fire, ambulance** ( ☎ 911)
**Police (nonemergency)** ( ☎ 877-275-5273)
**Rape Crisis Line** ( ☎ 213-626-3393)
**Rape Treatment Center** ( ☎ 310-319-4000)

## HOLIDAYS

**New Year's Day** January 1
**Martin Luther King Jr Day** third Monday in January
**Presidents' Day** third Monday in February

**Easter** a Friday and Sunday in March or April
**Memorial Day** last Monday in May
**Independence Day** July 4
**Labor Day** first Monday in September
**Columbus Day** second Monday in October
**Veterans' Day** November 11
**Thanksgiving** fourth Thursday in November
**Christmas Day** December 25

## INTERNET

Most hotels and some motels are equipped with data ports; better hotels offer high-speed internet access. Internet cafés and business centers, such as 24-hour branches of **FedEx Kinko's** ( ☎ 800-254-6567; www .fedexkinkos.com), are common. Logging on at public libraries is free, but may require signing up in person; some branches now provide free wi-fi for laptop users.

In addition to the LA links you'll find at Lonely Planet's website (www.lonelyplanet.com), the following may also be helpful:
**@LA** (www.at-la.com) All things LA.
**BlackNLA** (www.blacknla.com) Comprehensive info for African-Americans.
**Calendar Live** (www.calendarlive.com) *LA Times* list of arts and culture events
**Daily Candy** (www.dailycandy.com) Little bites of the stylish LA scene.
**LA.com** (www.la.com) Hip shopping, dining and nightlife guide.
**LA Inc** (www.visitlosangeles.info) Official website for the LA Convention & Visitors Bureau.
**LA Weekly** (www.laweekly.com) Updates on movies, galleries and theaters.
**Latino LA** (www.latinola.com) For Latino arts and entertainment.

## MONEY

For exchange rates, see the inside front cover of this guide. Meals per person per day will run $25 and up, hotel stays $100 and up, and public transportation within the city about $5 a day. Taxis can run much higher.

## TELEPHONE

US cell phones typically operate on CDMA. The only phones that work in North America are international triband models, operating on GSM 1900 as well as on GSM 900/1800. If you have such a phone, check with your service provider about use in the US.

### COUNTRY & CITY CODES

All California phone numbers consist of a three-digit area code followed by a seven-digit local number. For a number within the same area code, just dial the seven-digit number. If you are calling long distance, dial ☎ 1 plus the three-digit area code plus the seven-digit number. Toll-free numbers start with ☎ 800, ☎ 866, ☎ 877 or ☎ 888.
**Anaheim** ( ☎ 714)
**Beverly Hills, Culver City, Malibu, Santa Monica, South Bay** ( ☎ 310, 424)
**Burbank & San Fernando Valley** ( ☎ 818)
**Downtown LA** ( ☎ 213)
**Hollywood, Los Feliz, Mid-City, Silver Lake** ( ☎ 323)
**Pasadena & San Gabriel Valley** ( ☎ 626)

## USEFUL PHONE NUMBERS

**International direct dial tone** (☎ 011)
**International operator** (☎ 00)
**Local directory inquiries** (☎ 411)
**Operator** (☎ 0)
**Time** (☎ area code-853-1212)
**Toll-free directory inquiries** (☎ 1-800-555-1212)
**Weather** (☎ 213-554-1212)

## TIPPING

**Bars** 15%; minimum tip $1 per order
**Hotel porters** $1 to $2 per item
**Restaurants** 15% to 20%; tip may be included as a 'service charge' on bill for large groups
**Taxis** 10%
**Valet Parking** $2

## TOURIST INFORMATION

The main tourist offices:
**Downtown Los Angeles Visitor Information Center** (Map pp126–7, C4; ☎ 213-689-8822; 685 S Figueroa; ⊙ 8:30am-5pm Mon-Fri) Between 7th St and Wilshire.
**Hollywood Visitor Information Center** (Map pp40–1, C3; ☎ 323-467-6412; Hollywood & Highland, 6801 Hollywood Blvd; ☎ 10am-10pm Mon-Sat, 10am-7pm Sun)
**Los Angeles Convention and Visitors Bureau** (☎ 213-624-7300, 800-228-2452; www.lacvb.com) Provides maps, brochures, lodging information plus tickets to theme parks and attractions.

Other tourist offices:
**Beverly Hills Conference & Visitors Bureau** (Map pp84–5, H4; ☎ 310-248-1015, 800-345-2210; www.beverlyhillsbehere.com; 239 S Beverly Dr, Beverly Hills; ⊙ 8:30am-5pm Mon-Fri)

**Pasadena Convention & Visitors Bureau** (Map pp146–7, D3; ☎ 626-795-9311, 800-307-7977; www.pasadenacal.com; 171 S Los Robles Ave, Pasadena; ⊙ 8am-5pm Mon-Fri, currently closed Sat)
**Santa Monica Visitor Information Kiosk** (Map pp96–7, B4; Palisades Park, 1400 Ocean Ave; ⊙ 9am-5pm summer, 10am-4pm winter)
**Santa Monica Visitors Center** (Map pp96–7, C5; ☎ 310-393-7593, 800-544-5319; www.santamonica.com; 1920 Main St, Suite B; ⊙ 9am-6pm)
**West Hollywood Convention & Visitors Bureau** (Map p63, C3; ☎ 310-289-2525; www.visitwesthollywood.com; 8687 Melrose Ave, Suite M38, inside Pacific Design Center; ⊙ 8:30am-5:30pm Mon-Fri)

## TRAVELERS WITH DISABILITIES

Under current law, public buildings, restrooms and transportation (buses, trains and taxis) are required to be wheelchair accessible. Larger hotels and motels have rooms designed for guests with a disability. Listings in this book that are wheelchair friendly are indicated by the ⅙ icon. Telephone companies are required to provide relay operators for the hearing impaired. Guide dogs may legally be brought into restaurants, hotels and other businesses.

For paratransit and door-to-door services, contact **Access Services Incorporated** (☎ 800-827-0829; www.asila.org). Check with individual car rental agencies for hand-controlled vehicles or vans with wheelchair lifts. **Wheelers** ( ☎ 800-456-1371; www .wheelersvanrentals.com) specializes in these vehicles. You must have a permit for parking at blue-colored curbs and specially designated spots in public lots.

If you need assistance in LA, contact **LA County Commission on** **Disabilities** ( ☎ 213-974-1053, TTY 213-974-1707). The **Society for Accessible Travel & Hospitality** (SATH; ☎ 212-447-7284; www.sath.org) publishes accessibility guides and a quarterly magazine, *Open World*, for travelers with disabilities.

# >INDEX

*See also separate subindexes for See (p205), Shop (p206), Eat (p206), Drink (p207) and Play (p208).*

000 map pages

## ⦿ SEE

## DRINK